LUXURY HOTELS

EUROPE

edited by Martin Nicholas Kunz

teNeues

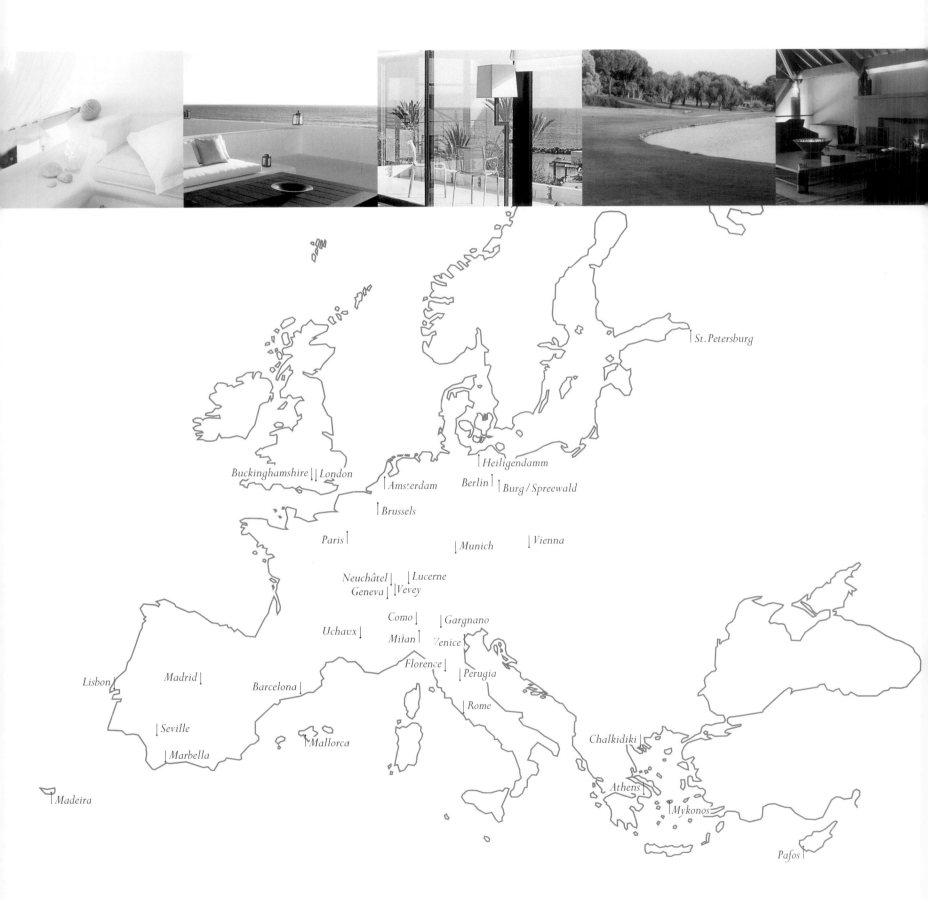

Buckinghamshire | London

Amsterdam

Brussels

Paris

Heiligendamm

Berlin | Burg / Spreewald

Munich

Vienna

St. Petersburg

Neuchâtel | Lucerne
Geneva | Vevey

Como | Gargnano

Uchaux | Milan | Venice

Florence | Perugia

Lisbon

Madrid

Barcelona

Rome

Seville

Mallorca

Chalkidiki

Marbella

Athens

Mykonos

Madeira

Pafos

Luxury Hotels Europe

Luxury is no Luxury

Luxury hotels, unsurprisingly, suggest a certain element of dreaming. However, it is interesting to note that the original term came from Latin and meant "twisted". It was only in the 17th century that the word acquired its current connotation of extravagance, exclusivity, as well as excessiveness and opulence. In the presence of so much freedom of interpretation, there is plenty of room for heated argument regarding sense and content, as has been demonstrated by countless philosophical, scientific and historical treatises.

Obviously, judging a particular subject is a matter of perspective. For someone living on the subsistence level, luxury might provoke envy and a lack of understanding, yet when seen from the viewpoint of art history and the social sciences, on the other hand, forms of luxury demonstrate the high level of achievement of which human-kind was and is capable. In earlier eras, expressions of luxury usually took the form of residences, church buildings, but also gravesites. Today, the focus has shifted somewhat. Globally active companies, and, in the meantime, the public sector as well, try to symbolise their power and attain a bit of immortality by setting striking signs of the times.

Yet even luxury items not carved from stone, such as luxury automobiles, yachts or luxury bathing facilities, clearly demonstrate what is possible in terms of technology and design. Even though these items are not absolute necessities, they are still intellectual proof of the "state of the art" in their respective time of creation. Along this vein, luxury hotels are also valuable indicators of the achievements of which nations, cities or outstanding regions are capable. And, incidentally—lest we forget—these lavish addresses are attractive buildings filled with fascination and surprises, in which one can live pleasantly.

Luxury—an ambivalent phenomenon, partly because it is only appreciated in a monoculture, as an absolute. The word is connected with an expected behaviour with regard to its extraordinary, unique, unforgettable and exclusive nature; that is, everything that—at the highest level—contradicts schematisation of any kind. As such, the spatial components serve only as the scaffolding upon which the various activities, encounters and mutual perceptions take place, the frame for a picture, a dream of sorts, in whose midst the guest experiences. A stage. But woe betide you if the surroundings are identified as a stage set! The opposite is expected: authenticity, a fine distillate of the environment quality and location-specific lifestyle.

All of this presents a great challenge to the management and staff, on the one hand, and of course to the architects and designers on the other. They must take the performance specifications for a smoothly functioning luxury hotel and implement them in such a way that the relationship to the location, its materials, colors and formats can be recognized as identifying parameters, and achieved with the highest level of craftsmanship and design.

Thus, architecture forms the backdrop for reception, lounging, pampering, enjoyment, relaxation, and communication—for everything that counters one's hectic, every-day routine. People can decompress here, renew their strength, experience fascination. In this regard, luxury hotels are accommodations of the most comfortable kind, whereby it is worthwhile to distinguish between those that follow formal criteria to solely create a piece of service real estate, and those that have subscribed to the goal of "true luxury".

The latter is the subject of this book, which presents examples of a contemporary culture of the extraordinary and, at the same time, a plea for the priority of hospitality. "Great" names, as well as lesser known "jewels", adorn the following pages in a collection of traditional and contemporary places of refuge—all in the highest of quality. Oscar Wilde willingly admitted to his very "simple" taste: just the best of everything! He would have enjoyed this collection of insider tips—and not only because this type of luxury does not even cost a fortune. .

Professor Axel Müller-Schöll
Chair for Interior Decorating of the Department of Design
University of Art and Design, Burg Giebichenstein, Halle (Saale)/Germany

Luxus ist kein Luxus

Natürlich haben Luxushotels auch etwas mit Träumen zu tun. Interessant ist allerdings, dass der ursprüngliche Begriff aus dem Lateinischen stammte und „verrenkt" ausdrückte. Erst im 17. Jahrhundert erhielt das Wort seine heutige Bedeutung von Üppigkeit, Kostbarkeit, aber auch von Schwelgerei und Verschwendung. Bei soviel Interpretationsfreiheit lässt sich leidenschaftlich über Sinn und Inhalte streiten, was schon die zahlreichen philosophischen, wissenschaftlichen und geschichtlichen Abhandlungen beweisen.

Ganz offensichtlich kommt es auf den Blickwinkel an, mit dem man das jeweilige Sujet beurteilt. Vom Existenzminimum aus betrachtet mag Luxus Neid und Unverständnis auslösen, aus der Perspektive der Kunstgeschichte und Gesellschaftswissenschaften zeigen die luxuriösen Ausprägungen dagegen, zu welchen Spitzenleistungen Menschen im Stande waren und sind. In früheren Epochen handelte es sich bei üppigen Ausdrücken der Zeit meist um Residenzen, Kirchenbauwerke, aber auch um Begräbnisstätten. Heute hat sich dies ein wenig verlagert. Global agierende Unternehmen und bisweilen auch die öffentliche Hand versuchen ihre Macht und auch ein wenig Unsterblichkeit mit markanten Zeitzeichen zu symbolisieren.

Doch auch nicht in Stein gehaute Luxusartikel, wie etwa Luxusautomobile, Luxusjachten oder Luxusbäder zeigen eindrücklich, was technisch und gestalterisch möglich ist. Auch wenn dies alles Dinge sind, die keiner lebensnotwendig „braucht", so sind sie doch geistiges Zeugnis über den „Stand der Dinge" in der jeweiligen Zeit ihrer Entstehung. In diesem Sinne sind auch Luxushotels kostbare Indikatoren dafür, zu welchen Höchstleistungen Nationen, Metropolen oder herausragende Landschaftsregionen im Stande sind. Und ganz nebenbei – das soll hier keinesfalls vergessen werden – sind die Edeladressen anziehende, mit Faszination und Überraschungen beladene Häuser, in denen sich ein angenehmes Leben führen lässt.

Luxus – ein ambivalentes Phänomen, auch weil er nur in Reinkultur goutiert wird, als Absolutum. Denn mit diesem Begriff verbindet sich auch eine Erwartungshaltung im Bezug auf Außerordentlichkeit, Einmaligkeit, Unvergesslichkeit und Exklusivität. Also alles das, was sich – auf höchstem Niveau – gegen jede Art von Schematisierung ins Felde führen ließe. Dabei bildet die räumliche Komponente lediglich das Traggerüst, in dem sich die verschiedenen Handlungen, Begegnungen und die gegenseitige Wahrnehmung verorten, als Passepartout für ein Bild, einen Traum gewissermaßen, in dessen Mitte sich der Gast erlebt. Eine Bühne. Ja, aber wehe wenn die Umgebung als Bühnendekoration zu erkennen ist! Erwartet wird das Gegenteil: Authentizität, ein feines Destillat der Umgebungsqualität und der ortspezifischen Lebensart.

Dies alles stellt eine große Herausforderung dar, einerseits an Management und Personal, andererseits natürlich auch an die Architekten und Designer. Sie haben das Lastenheft der Funktionsanforderungen eines reibungslos funktionierenden Nobeletablissements so umzusetzen, dass der Ortsbezug, dessen Materialien, Farben und Formate als identitätsstiftende Parameter lesbar sind und gleichfalls in ihrer höchsten Form handwerklich wie gestalterisch umgesetzt werden.

Die Architektur bildet also den Hintergrund für das Empfangen, Verweilen, Umsorgen, Genießen, Ausruhen, Kommunizieren – für alles, was sich der Hektik und der Routine des Alltages entgegensetzen lässt. Hier lässt sich Dekompression erleben, Kraft schöpfen, Faszination spüren. In diesem Sinne sind Luxushotels Beherbergungsstätten der angenehmsten Art, wobei es sich zu unterscheiden lohnt zwischen denjenigen, die den formalen Kriterien folgend lediglich eine Dienstleistungsimmobilie erzeugen und denjenigen, die sich dem Ziel des „wahren Luxus" verschrieben haben.

Um letztere geht es in dem vorliegenden Buch, es sind Beispiele für eine heute existierende Kultur des Außerordentlichen und gleichermaßen ein Plädoyer für das Primat der Gastlichkeit. „Große" Namen wie weniger bekannte „Juwelen" bilden auf den folgenden Seiten eine ungewöhnliche Kollektion traditioneller und neuer – aber alle auf höchstem Niveau gestalteter Refugien. Oscar Wilde bekannte sich zu seinem ganz „einfachen" Geschmack: Von allem nur das Beste! Er hätte an dieser Geheimtippsammlung seine Freude gehabt und nicht nur, weil diese Art von Luxus nicht einmal gleich ein Vermögen kostet.

Professor Axel Müller-Schöll
Lehrstuhl für Design und Innenarchitektur an der Burg Giebichenstein, Halle
University of Art and Design, Burg Giebichenstein, Halle (Saale)/Germany

Le luxe n'est pas un luxe

Il va de soi que les hôtels de luxe ont quelque chose à voir avec les rêves. Il est cependant intéressant de constater que le terme était initialement originaire du latin et signifiait « luxé ». Ce n'est qu'au XVIIe siècle que le mot obtint son sens actuel d'exubérance, de grande valeur, mais aussi de faste et de gaspillage. Etant donné cette grande liberté d'interprétation, on peut passionnément discuter du sens et des contenus, ce qui est déjà souligné par le grand nombre de traités et études philosophiques, scientifiques et historiques.

Cela dépend très manifestement de la perspective avec laquelle on aborde le sujet en question. Du point de vue du minimum vital, le luxe peut bien entraîner l'envie et l'incompréhension, tandis que, de la perspective de l'histoire de l'art et des sciences sociales, les empreintes luxurieuses témoignent par contre des grandes performances que pouvaient réaliser les êtres humains. Dans les anciennes époques, les expressions fastueuses se rapportaient le plus souvent à des résidences, édifices de l'Eglise, mais aussi à des lieux de sépulture. Aujourd'hui, cette conception a quelque peu changé. Les entreprises présentent dans le monde entier ainsi que, parfois, les pouvoirs publics essaient de symboliser leur pouvoir et, un peu aussi, leur immortalité avec des signes prégnants du temps.

On peut cependant aussi dire que des articles de luxes non sculptés dans la pierre, comme par exemple les automobiles de luxe, les yachts de luxe ou les salles de bain de luxe montrent de manière remarquable ce qui est possible sur le plan technique et du design. Même s'il s'agit là de choses dont personne n'a vraiment besoin pour vivre, ce sont bien des témoins spirituels de « l'état des choses » à l'époque de leur création. Dans ce sens, les hôtels de luxe sont également des indicateurs précieux des grandes performances dont peuvent se prévaloir des nations, métropoles ou régions et paysages éminents. Et, tout juste en passant, ce que nous ne voulons ici en aucun cas oublier, les nobles adresses sont des établissements attrayants. fascinants et pleins de surprises dans lesquels la vie est « douce ».

Le luxe – Phénomène ambivalent, également parce qu'on n'y goutte qu'à cent pour cent, comme valeur absolue. En effet, ce terme implique aussi une certaine attente en ce qui concerne le caractère extraordinaire, unique, inoubliable et exclusif. Et donc tout ce qu'on pourrait – au plus haut niveau – utiliser comme argument contre toute sorte de schématisation. La composante spatiale ne constitue ici que la charpente support abritant les différentes actions, rencontres et les perceptions réciproques, passe-partout pour une image, d'une certaine manière un rêve au centre duquel l'hôte s'appréhende. Une scène. Oui, mais gare si on saisit l'environnement comme décoration de scène ! On s'attend plutôt au contraire : authenticité, un distillat fin de la qualité de l'environnement et du mode de vie spécifique local.

Tout ceci est un grand défi d'une part pour le management et le personnel, et d'autre part naturellement pour les architectes et designers. Ils se doivent de mettre en œuvre le cahier de charges des exigences fonctionnelles d'un noble établissement fonctionnant parfaitement de manière à ce que la connexion avec la localité, les matériaux utilisés ainsi que les couleurs et les formats puissent tenir lieu de paramètres identificateurs et puissent de la même manière être réalisés aussi bien sur le plan artisanal que conceptionnel sous sa forme la plus éminente.

L'architecture constitue donc l'arrière-plan pour l'accueil, le séjour, le fait de (se faire) choyer, la jouissance, le repos, la communication, et donc pour tout ce qui s'oppose à la fébrilité et la routine du quotidien. On peut vivre ici la décompression, recharger ses batteries, ressentir la fascination. Ainsi vus, les hôtels de luxe sont des établissements d'hébergement extrêmement agréables, ceci étant entendu qu'il vaut la peine de faire la distinction entre ceux qui créent simplement un immeuble de prestation de services conformément aux critères formels et ceux qui se sont vraiment dédiés au « luxe véritable ».

Le présent livre traite de ce dernier ; il comprend des exemples d'une culture de l'extraordinaire que l'on vit aujourd'hui et constitue de même un plaidoyer pour le primat de l'hospitalité. Aussi bien des « grands » noms que des « joyaux » moins célèbres constituent sur les pages qui suivent une collection insolite de traditionnels et nouveaux refuges pourtant tous aménagés au plus haut niveau. Oscar Wilde confessa son goût tout « simple » : le nec plus ultra seulement ! Il aurait eu un grand plaisir à consulter ce recueil de « tuyaux », et ce pas seulement parce que ce genre de luxe ne coûte même pas une fortune.

Professeur Axel Müller-Schöll
Chaire d'architecture d'intérieur à la faculté de Design
University of Art and Design, Burg Giebichenstein, Halle (Saale)/Germany

El lujo no lo es tal

Obviamente, los hoteles de lujo también tienen que ver con los sueños. No obstante, resulta interesante que el término original proviniera del latín y expresara "torcido". Hasta el siglo 17 no alcanzó el vocablo su significado actual de suntuosidad y carácter valioso, aunque también de derroche y despilfarro. Ante tanta libertad de interpretación puede discutirse apasionadamente sobre sentido y contenido, lo que ya demuestran numerosos tratados filosóficos, científicos e históricos.

Todo depende obviamente del punto de vista con que valore el tema correspondiente. Visto desde el umbral de la pobreza, el lujo podría generar envidia e incomprensión, por el contrario, desde la perspectiva de la historia del arte y la sociología, las connotaciones de lujo muestran el máximo nivel de logro que estaban, y están, en condiciones de alcanzar las personas. En épocas pasadas, las suntuosas expresiones del momento estaban generalmente relacionadas con residencias y edificios del clero, pero también con tumbas. Esto ha cambiado algo en la actualidad. Las empresas que funcionan globalmente, y también el sector público en ocasiones, utilizan signos temporales notorios para intentar simbolizar su poder y algo también su inmortalidad.

Pero los artículos de lujo no labrados en piedra, como por ejemplo los automóviles, yates o baños de lujo, muestran también claramente lo que resulta posible a nivel técnico y de creatividad. A pesar de que todo esto son cosas que nadie "necesita" imperiosamente para vivir, sí son no obstante un certificado mental del "estado de las cosas" en el momento puntual de su origen. En este sentido, los hoteles de lujo son también indicadores valiosos sobre el máximo nivel de logro que están en condiciones de alcanzar los países, metrópolis o regiones comarcales destacadas. Y dicho sea de paso, y que no se olvide aquí en ningún caso, los alojamientos nobles son casas atractivas y cargadas de fascinación y sorpresa donde puede desarrollarse una vida agradable.

El lujo es un fenómeno ambivalente, también porque sólo es apreciado como algo absoluto en una cultura pura, pues este concepto entronca también con una actitud de expectativa en relación con lo extraordinario, único, inolvidable y exclusivo. Todo aquello pues que pudiera alegarse contra cualquier tipo de carácter sistemático al máximo nivel. A este respecto, el componente espacial sólo constituye el soporte donde se emplazan las diferentes acciones, encuentros y percepciones recíprocas, una especie de llave maestra para una imagen o sueño que el cliente experimenta como actor principal. Un escenario. ¡Sí, pero ojo cuando el ambiente ha de percibirse como la decoración de un escenario! Lo que se espera es justo lo contrario: Autenticidad, un fino producto destilado de calidad ambiental y estilo de vida específico del lugar.

Todo esto constituye un gran desafío; por un lado, en cuanto a gestión y personal, y por otro, también obviamente en lo que respecta a arquitectos y diseñadores. Usted tiene el pliego de condiciones de convertir de tal modo los requisitos funcionales de un noble establecimiento que funcione perfectamente, que la compra del lugar, sus materiales, colores y formatos sean legibles como parámetros que les confieren una identidad, y transformados igualmente en su máxima expresión artesanal y creativa.

La arquitectura constituye pues el marco para la recepción, estancia, cuidado, disfrute, descanso y comunicación; para todo que pueda oponerse al estrés y la rutina diaria. Aquí puede experimentarse descompresión, creación de fuerza y sentimiento de fascinación. En este sentido, los hoteles de lujo son lugares de hospedaje del tipo más agradable, mereciendo la pena distinguir entre aquellos que, siguiendo exclusivamente criterios formales, constituyen una entidad de servicio y los que se adscriben al objetivo del "lujo auténtico".

El presente libro trata de la segunda opción, contiene ejemplos de una cultura actual donde prima lo extraordinario y, del mismo modo, un alegato sobre la primacía de la hospitalidad. En las siguientes páginas aparece una insólita colección de refugios tradicionales y nuevos formada por "grandes" nombres y "joyas" menos conocidas, pero todos con el máximo nivel de creatividad. En relación con su "modesto" gusto, Oscar Wilde confesó: ¡Extraer sólo lo mejor de todo! Él habría celebrado esta colección de recomendaciones secretas, y no sólo por no costar una fortuna esta clase de lujo.

Profesor Axel Müller-Schöll
Cátedra de Decoración Interior en la Facultad de Diseño
University of Art and Design, Burg Giebichenstein, Halle (Saale)/Germany

Hotel Astoria

St. Petersburg, Russia

Paying tribute to a hotel's location is the general principle of Rocco Forte Group luxury hotels. Accordingly, the Astoria Hotel exudes the same aura possessed by St. Petersburg when it was the original capital of the Tsarist empire. Undisputedly the most superb address on the Square, the hotel offers not only all of the extras one would expect of a luxury hotel, including a gourmetrestaurant and classy bar. Perhaps even more impressive is how several small details in the over 200 rooms reveal erstwhile Russian craftsmanship, while the polished, white and grey marble from Italy lends the bathrooms that famous sumptuous shine. Incidentally, the higher the accommodation category, the more lavish are the interior and furnishings. Not to be topped: the five presidential suites that shimmer in shades of purple like royal chambers, filled with antiques and gold faceted jewellery.

Tribut zu zollen an den Ort, der sie umgibt, gehört zum durchgängigen Prinzip der Luxushotels der Rocco Forte Gruppe. Dementsprechend verströmt das Astoria Hotel selbst jene Aura, die St. Petersburg als ursprüngliche Hauptstadt des Zarenreiches innewohnt. Als unbestritten feinste Adresse am Platz offeriert das Hotel dabei nicht nur all die zu erwartenden Extras einer Nobelherberge, Gourmetrestaurant und edle Bar inklusive. Viel bemerkenswerter erscheint, wie in vielen kleinen Details in den über 200 Räumen alte russische Manufakturen zum Vorschein kommen, während der polierte, weißgraue Marmor aus Italien den Badezimmern den bekannt luxuriösen Glanz verleiht. Je höher die Kategorie der Unterbringung, umso üppiger fällt im übrigen Interieur und Ausstattung aus. Nicht mehr zu überbieten: die fünf Präsidentensuiten, die wie königliche Gemächer in purpurnen Farben schillern, angefüllt mit Antiquitäten und in Gold gefassten Schmuckstücken.

L'un des principes généraux des hôtels du luxe du groupe Rocco Forte est de payer un tribut sur leur site. C'est ainsi que l'hôtel Astoria bénéficie de l'aura qui se trouve à St. Petersbourg, ancienne capitale du royaume des tsars. Cet hôtel, situé incontestablement à une adresse de premier choix, offre non seulement tous les extra attendus dans un hébergement noble, mais également un restaurant gourmet et des bars de première classe. Il convient de remarquer combien l'ancienne tradition de manufacture russe apparaît dans de nombreux détails des 200 pièces de l'hôtel, tandis que le marbre italien poli, aux tons de blanc et de gris, donne aux salles de bains une brillance luxueuse typique du marbre. Plus la catégorie de logement est élevée, plus l'intérieur et les équipements sont somptueux. Il est difficile de faire mieux que les cinq suites présidentielles, qui, comme des appartements royaux, brillent de teintes pourpres, regorgent d'antiquités et de décorations couvertes de dorures.

Los hoteles de lujo del grupo Rocco Forte tienen como principio básico rendir tributo al lugar que los circunda. Por esta razón, el hotel Astoria está rodeado de ese aura que caracteriza a San Petersburgo como capital original del imperio de los zares. Siendo sin lugar a dudas el destino más fino del lugar, el hotel no sólo ofrece todas las características especiales que se esperan de una residencia noble, incluido restaurante gourmet y bar señorial. Llama más la atención la forma en que se manifiestan viejos productos de fabricación rusa, reflejados en muchos pequeños detalles en las más de 200 habitaciones, mientras que el mármol gris-blanco pulimentado proveniente de Italia confiere a los cuartos de baño el famoso brillo lujoso. A mayor categoría del alojamiento, más fastuoso es también el interior y el mobiliario. Imposible de superar: las cinco suites presidenciales que relucen como aposentos reales en colores púrpura, repletas de antigüedades y adornos diseñados en oro.

A direct view of St. Isaac's Cathedral is just one of the attractions this hotel has to offer. The beds make an impression with their hand-made linens and embroidered monograms.

Die direkte Sicht auf die St. Isaak Kathedrale ist nur ein Reiz, den das Hotel bietet. Die Betten überraschen mit handgewebtem Leinen und eingearbeiteten Monogrammen.

La vue directe sur la cathédrale St. Isaak est l'une des nombreuses attractions de l'hôtel. Les lits aux draps de lin tissés main avec des applications de monogrammes provoqueront l'étonnement des visiteurs.

La vista directa de la catedral de St. Isaak es sólo uno de los atractivos que ofrece el hotel. Las camas sorprenden por el lino tejido a mano y los monogramas insertados.

The view into the Rachmaninov Suite reveals pure luxury. Evidently, thoughts flow even more freely at spots like this desk.

Der Blick in die Rachmaninow-Suite offenbart puren Luxus. An solchen Plätzen wie diesem Schreibtisch fließen die Gedanken wohl noch angeregter.

Si vous jetez un coup d'œil dans la suite de Rachmaninov, vous découvrirez le pur luxe. Tout visiteur assis à ce bureau, verra croître l'inspiration de ses pensées.

La vista de la suite Rachmaninow manifiesta puro lujo. En lugares como este escritorio, los pensamientos fluyen con más estimulación aún si cabe.

In the lobby lounge, the hotel serves a breakfast buffet, where samovars are a must. Flowering Callas decorate the table settings in the restaurant. Both rooms play with a 20's era theme.

In der Lobby-Lounge serviert das Hotel das Frühstück als Büffet, wozu Samoware zwangsläufig dazugehören. Blühende Callas verschönern derweil die gedeckten Tische im Restaurant. Beide Räume spielen mit dem Stil der 20er Jahre.

Dans la salle à manger, l'hôtel propose un petit-déjeuner sous forme de buffet où l'on trouve immanquablement les samovars, pendant que les callas en fleur ornent les tables du restaurant. Dans ces deux pièces, on rencontre des effets de style des années 20.

El hotel sirve el desayuno en el salón del vestíbulo en forma de buffet, para lo que se requiere inevitablemente Samoware. Callas florecientes embellecen entretanto las mesas cubiertas del restaurante. Ambas lugares armonizan con el estilo de los años 20.

Stoke Park Club
Buckinghamshire, UK

From a distance the palatial building of the Stoke Park Club appears to be a miniature of the White House. However the hoisted Union Jack clearly shows that British style dominates here: The Stoke Park Club is considered to be the oldest Country Golf Club in the country. The house and park grounds look back onto a century-old history. This venerable ambience characterized by the luxury of a reputable Members Club houses 21 individual suites furnished with an array of antique furniture and old prints and works of art on the walls. A treat for the eyes is offered by the marble bathrooms with their free-standing bathtubs. Since 2002 the hotel has been able to entice guests with one of the largest spas in Great Britain. not to mention the park originating back to the 18th century. Adding to the history of the house are numerous filmings: two James Bond films and "Notting Hill" featuring club member Hugh Grant.

Von weitem erscheint das palastartige Gebäude des Stoke Park Club fast wie eine Miniatur des Weißen Hauses. Doch der geflaggte Union Jack macht gleich deutlich, dass hier britischer Stil die Vormacht behauptet. Mehr noch: Der Stoke Park Club gilt als der älteste Country Golf Club des Landes, Haus und Parkgelände blicken auf eine Jahrhunderte alte Geschichte zurück. In diesem ehrwürdigen Ambiente, vom Luxus eines hoch angesehenen Member Clubs geprägt, stehen eine überschaubare Anzahl von 21 individuellen Suiten zur Verfügung, ausgestattet mit einem Heer von antiken Möbeln und alten Drucken an den Wänden. Eine Augenweide geradezu, die marmornen Badezimmer mit ihren frei stehenden Wannen. Seit 2002 lockt zudem eines der großzügigsten Spa-Angebote in ganz Großbritannien, vom original angelegten Park aus dem 18. Jahrhundert ganz zu schweigen. Dass hier sogar zwei James Bond Streifen und „Notting Hill" mit Clubmitglied Hugh Grant gefilmt wurden. gehört zu den vielen Anekdoten des Hauses.

De loin, le bâtiment en forme de palace du Stoke Park Club ressemble fortement à la Maison Blanche en miniature. Le Union Jack qui le pavoise indique toutefois et tout de suite, sans ambiguïté, que c'est le style britannique qui prédomine ici. Plus encore, le Stoke Park Club est considéré comme le Country Golf Club le plus ancien du pays ; le bâtiment et le parc ont une histoire de plusieurs centaines d'années. Ce cadre respectable caractérisé par le luxe d'un Member's Club de haute réputation offre un nombre réduit de 21 suites individuelles équipées d'une armée de meubles antiques et décorées avec des anciens imprimés et autres ouvrages classiques sur les murs. Les salles de bain en marbre, avec leurs baignoires isolées, sont un régal pour les yeux. Depuis 2002, son offre attrayante comprend en outre un des plus grands spas de Grande-Bretagne, sans parler du parc original érigé au XVIIIe siècle. Exemples tirés des nombreuses anecdotes de l'établissement : deux films James Bond et « Notting Hill » avec Hugh Grant, qui est membre du club, ont été filmés ici.

Visto de lejos, el edificio con aspecto de palacio del Stoke Park Club casi parece una miniatura de la Casa Blanca. Pero la Union Jack (bandera del Reino Unido) deja bien claro desde el principio que el estilo británico conserva aquí la hegemonía. Más aún si cabe: El Stoke Park Club está considerado el club de golf más antiguo del país; la casa y el terreno del parque echan la vista atrás a una vieja historia de siglos. En este venerable ambiente, marcado por el lujo de un club de miembros de alta consideración, existe un número controlable de 21 suites individuales disponibles, equipadas con una multitud de muebles usados y viejas estampas y obras en las paredes. Los cuartos de baño de mármol con sus bañeras aisladas constituyen un verdadero deleite para la vista. Desde 2002 sirve además como atracción una de las ofertas de balneario más jugosas de toda Gran Bretaña, sin hacer alusión al parque original construido el siglo 18. Entre las muchas anécdotas de la casa se cuentan el rodaje de dos cintas de James Bond y la película "Notting Hill", en la que actuó el miembro del club Hugh Grant.

Marble wherever you look—in the bathrooms. Even in the rooms themselves: grandness itself right up to the purple color surroundings.

Marmor, wohin das Auge schaut, in den Badezimmern. Selbst die Zimmer: herrschaftlich bis in die purpurne Farbgebung hinein.

Le marbre partout où on regarde dans les salles de bain. Et les chambres sont féodales dans tous les détails, même jusqu'à leur couleur pourpre.

Hay mármol allí donde se posa la vista, como en los cuartos de baño. Las habitaciones desprenden señorialidad hasta adentrarse en el colorido purpúreo.

Time-honoring does not have to mean old-fashioned—quite the opposite: the new spa awaits guests to pamper them offering an array of treatments and complete relaxation.

Altehrwürdig muss nicht verstaubt bedeuten. Im Gegenteil: Das neue Spa wartet mit allen Raffinessen der heutigen Zeit für die körperliche Pflege und Entspannung auf.

Vénérable ne doit pas forcément signifier désuet. Au contraire, le nouveau spa offre tous les raffinements contemporains pour le soin corporel et la relaxation.

Venerable no tiene que significar empolvado. Al contrario: Con todos sus refinamientos actuales, el balneario le espera para el tratamiento corporal y relajación.

Knightsbridge
London, UK

Out of Africa and into the centre of London. Behind its classical façade, this intimate and endearing hotel unites the lifestyle of teatime and British society with an ethnographic globetrotter and art-lover's passion for collecting. Sculptures resembling termite hills are just as much a part of the collection as are stools with zebra skins and ceramics with motifs from the Dark Continent. Through and through, the hotel bears the aesthetic mark of a young owner, designer Kit Kemp. No one room or suite resembles another. Each possesses a decidedly individual design, yet all are characterised by a fresh, modern English style. The absolute highlight: the bathrooms, done totally in polished black granite. Even a study is open to guests. In short: a fine address and well-kept secret that one would only want to pass on to good friends.

Jenseits von Afrika und doch mitten in London. Hinter der klassizistischen Hausfront vereint dieses intime wie sympathische Hotel das Lebensgefühl von Teatime und britischer Society mit der Sammelleidenschaft eines ethnographischen Globetrotters und Kunstliebhabers. Termitenhügelähnliche Skulpturen gehören genauso dazu wie Hocker mit Zebrafellen und Keramiken mit Motiven vom Schwarzen Kontinent. Das Hotel trägt durch und durch die ästhetische Handschrift seines jungen Besitzers, des Designers Kit Kemp. Kein Raum, keine Suite gleicht dem bzw. der anderen. Alle besitzen eine durchweg individuelle Gestaltung, die ein frischer wie moderner englischer Stil durchzieht. Deren absoluter Glanzpunkt: die ganz in poliertem schwarzen Granit gehaltenen Badezimmer. Selbst ein Bibliotheksraum steht den Gästen offen. Kurz gefasst: Eine feine und gut behütete Adresse, die man am liebsten nur guten Freunden weitergeben möchte.

Situé au-delà de l'Afrique, et pourtant au centre de Londres, derrière une façade de style classique, cet hôtel tant intime que sympathique combine une atmosphère britannique, de Teatime, avec la passion d'un globe-trotter ethnographe amoureux des objets d'art. On y trouve aussi bien des sculptures semblables à des monticules de termites que des tabourets en peau de zèbre ou des céramiques aux motifs typiques du continent noir. L'hôtel est signé de fond en comble par la main de son jeune propriétaire et designer, Kit Kemp. Aucune pièce, aucune suite ne ressemble à une autre. Toutes possèdent une décoration unique en son genre, dans un style anglais, frais et moderne. Un point de brillance absolue : le granit noir poli des salles de bains a été conservé. Il y a même une salle de bibliothèque ouverte aux visiteurs. En bref : voici une adresse raffinée et bien gardée qu'il convient de transmettre uniquement aux bons amis.

Más allá de África y sin embargo en el centro de Londres. Tras la clásica fachada de la casa, este hotel íntimo y simpático conjuga la sensibilidad vital de la hora del té y la sociedad británica con la pasión acumulada de un trotamundos etnográfico y amante del arte. Su mobiliario incluye, tanto esculturas similares a termiteros, como taburetes con pieles de cebra y cerámicas con motivos del continente negro. En cuanto al carácter estético, el hotel está impregnado por el sello de su joven propietario, el diseñador Kit Kemp. No hay ningún lugar o suite que sean idénticos. Todas tienen un diseño completamente particular, reflejado en un estilo inglés fresco y moderno. Su aspecto más destacado: Los cuartos de baño, conservados totalmente en granito negro pulido. Los clientes pueden disponer incluso de una sala de biblioteca. Resumiendo: Se trata de un lugar fino y protegido que sólo se revelaría a los mejores amigos.

Very British are the rooms. However, otherwise, primarily African themes dominate the hotel's interior.

Very british, die Zimmer. Ansonsten aber dominieren vor allem afrikanische Motive die Räume des Hotels.

Les pièces sont very british. Mais ce sont surtout les motifs africains qui dominent dans les salles de l'hôtel.

Las habitaciones tienen un carácter bastante británico. Por lo demás, el hotel está sin embargo dominado por motivos africanos sobre todo.

French sandstone frames the lobby fireplace. Bizarre sculptures decorate the area around the window there.

Französischer Sandstein umrahmt den Kamin in der Lobby. Bizarre Skulpturen dekorieren den Platz dort am Fenster.

Le grès français encadre la cheminée de la salle à manger. De curieuses sculptures décorent ce coin près de la fenêtre.

La chimenea del vestíbulo se halla enmarcada por piedra arenisca francesa. El lugar junto a la ventana está decorado con extravangantes esculturas.

A place of serenity away from the hectic pace of the British metropolis. The hotel study has room for relaxed hours spent with books, and perhaps even a cup of tea.

Ein Ort der Beruhigung vom hektischen Betrieb der britischen Metropole. Die Bibliothek des Hotels gibt Raum für entspannende Stunden mit Büchern, gerne mit einem Tee dazu.

Un lieu de repos, loin du stress de la métropole britannique : la bibliothèque de l'hôtel permet de se détendre en lisant, et pourquoi pas avec une tasse de thé.

Un lugar para descansar del bullicio estresante de la metrópoli británica. La biblioteca del hotel es un espacio habilitado para pasar horas relajadas en compañía de libros, y aderezadas con una taza de té.

Threadneedles

London, UK

In the heart of London's financial district stands a hotel which served as the sight of credit transactions in days gone by. Midland Bank had the building erected over 150 years ago to function as its representative seat in the British capital. As you can imagine, nowadays, a number of bankers stay here or visit "Bonds", the hotel restaurant, for a business lunch. The ostentatious foyer, with its decorated glass dome ceiling, is a popular meeting place in Threadneedles, as well as an architectural highlight. Yet when the establishment was modernized, care was taken not to overload guests with history in their rooms. All rooms are furnished in a contemporary, functional and subdued manner.

Im Herzen des Londoner Finanzdistrikts liegt ein Luxushotel, in dessen Gemäuer in der Vergangenheit selbst Kreditgeschäfte abgewickelt wurden. Vor 150 Jahren ließ es die Midland Bank als repräsentativen Sitz in der englischen Metropole bauen. Dass heute natürlich viele Banker hier übernachten oder mittags auf einen Business-Lunch ins Hotel-Restaurant „Bonds" vorbeischauen, versteht sich von selbst. Ein beliebter Treffpunkt und architektonisches Glanzstück des Threadneedles ist die pompöse Eingangshalle mit einem verzierten Glas-Kuppeldach. In den Zimmern achtete man bei der Modernisierung aber darauf, dass die Gäste nicht mit zu viel Historie überfrachtet werden, alle Räume sind zeitgemäß, funktional und zurückhaltend ausgestaltet.

Au cœur du district financier de Londres se trouve un hôtel de luxe dont les murailles abritèrent naguère des opérations de crédit. Il fut érigé il y a 150 ans par la Midland Bank qui voulait en faire son siège représentatif dans la métropole anglaise. Il va donc de soi que, aujourd'hui, un grand nombre de banquiers y passent la nuit ou se retrouvent à midi à « Bonds », le restaurant de l'hôtel, pour un déjeuner d'affaires. La pompeuse halle d'entrée avec son comble en dôme en verre orné est un point de rencontre aimé et le joyau architectural du Threadneedles. Lors de la modernisation des chambres, on a toutefois veillé à ce que les hôtes ne soient pas surchargés d'histoire. Toutes les pièces sont modernes, fonctionnelles et aménagées avec réserve.

En el corazón del distrito financiero de Londres se encuentra un hotel de lujo entre cuyas paredes se desarrollaron incluso operaciones de crédito en el pasado. El banco Midland lo mandó construir hace 150 años como emplazamiento representativo en la metrópoli inglesa. El hecho de que actualmente pernocten aquí muchos banqueros o se acerquen al mediodía para tomar un almuerzo de negocios en el hotel-restaurante "Bonds" es algo que se entiende por sí solo. El ostentoso hall de entrada, con su cúpula engalanada de cristal, constituye un popular lugar de encuentro y pieza maestra arquitectónica del Threadneedles. En el proceso de modernización se tuvo en cuenta no sobrecargar a los clientes con demasiada historia en las habitaciones. Todas las habitaciones son modernas, funcionales y discretas.

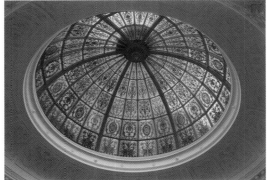

Leather armchairs and plenty of room for discussions can be found in the lobby. A large glass dome sheds light on the foyer.

Ledersessel und viel Raum für Gespräche bietet die Lobby. Licht spendet die große Glaskuppel.

Le lobby est équipé de fauteuils en cuir et offre beaucoup d'espace pour les conversations. Un grand dôme en verre l'inonde de lumière.

El vestíbulo dispone de butacas de cuero y mucho espacio para conversaciones. La iluminación proviene de una gran cúpula de cristal.

The rooms are decorated with a contemporary flair, and are wholly adapted to the needs of business travellers. Thus, large bathrooms are a hotel standard.

Die Zimmer sind modern gestaltet und ganz auf die Bedürfnisse von Geschäftsreisenden abgestimmt. Zum Standard im Hause zählen deshalb große Badezimmer.

Les chambres ont un aménagement moderne et parfaitement adapté aux besoins des V.R.P. C'est ainsi que des grandes salles de bain sont standard dans l'établissement.

Las habitaciones tienen un diseño moderno y se adaptan completamente a las necesidades de los viajeros de negocios. Los grandes cuartos de baño se cuentan por tanto entre las características generales de la casa.

Hotel Pulitzer

Amsterdam, The Netherlands

Façades with narrow parapets, decorative gables made of sandstone, and bright white transom windows with multiple panes provide Amsterdam's canal houses with their unique charm. No less than twenty-five of these canal houses dating from the 17th and 18th centuries along the Prinsengracht and Keizersgracht canals house the 230 rooms and suites of the Hotel Pulitzer. For 33 million dollars, the establishment, part of the Luxury Collection of the Starwood Group, was recently renovated, allowing modern interior and historical architecture to enter a successful partnership. Especially charming are the inner gardens with an original art deco glasshouse. And for guests arriving on their own boat, there are private slips.

Schmalbrüstige Fassaden, Schmuckgiebel aus Sandstein, vielfältig gegliederte, strahlend weiße Sprossenfenster machen den Charme der Amsterdamer Grachtenhäuser aus. Nicht weniger als fünfundzwanzig dieser Grachtenhäuser aus dem 17. und 18. Jahrhundert an Prinsengracht und Keizersgracht beherbergen die 230 Zimmer und Suiten des Hotel Pulitzer. Mit einem Aufwand von 33 Millionen Dollar wurde das Haus, das zur Luxury Collection der Starwood-Gruppe gehört, in jüngster Zeit renoviert, wobei modernes Interieur und historische Architektur eine gekonnte Verbindung eingehen. Ein besonderes Kleinod sind die Innengärten mit dem original Art-Déco-Glashaus. Für Gäste, die mit dem eigenen Boot anreisen, gibt es einen privaten Anleger.

Des façades étroites, des pignons décoratifs en grès, des fenêtres à barreaux agencées de manière multiple, au blanc étincelant font tout le charme des maisons sur pignons d'Amsterdam (les « Grachten »). Pas moins de vingt-cinq de ces maisons du XVIIe et du XVIIIe siècle situés sur le Prinsengracht et le Keizersgracht abritent les 230 chambres et les suites de l'hôtel Pulitzer. L'établissement, qui appartient à la Luxury Collection du groupe Starwood, a été récemment rénové avec un budget de 33 millions de dollars. L'intérieur moderne et l'architecture historique forment une alliance très réussie. Le point d'orgue est constitué par les jardins intérieurs avec la maison en verre typiquement art déco. Et pour les hôtes qui arrivent avec leur propre bateau, il existe un embarcadère privé.

Las casas de canales de Amsterdam adquieren su encanto en virtud de fachadas estrechas, frontispicio ornamental de piedra arenisca y ventanas de baquetilla distribuidas de forma variada e irradiando blancura. Las 230 habitaciones y suites del hotel Pulitzer se hallan distribuidas en al menos veinticinco de estas casas de canales del siglo 17 y 18, situadas concretamente en los canales Prensen y Keizer. El hotel, que pertenece a la colección de lujo del grupo Starwood, ha sido recientemente renovado invirtiéndose en ello 33 millones de dólares, y lográndose una acertada combinación entre un interior moderno y una arquitectura con carácter histórico. Los jardines interiores, con su invernadero original de estilo de arte deco, constituyen un tesoro especial. Y para los clientes que viajen con su propio barco existe un embarcadero privado.

On the famous Amsterdam canal belt stands the Pulitzer, composed of twenty-five of the typical canal houses.

Am berühmten Amsterdamer Grachtengürtel liegt das Pulitzer, das aus fünfundzwanzig der typischen Grachtenhäuser besteht.

Le Pulitzer est situé sur la célèbre ceinture des maisons sur pignons aux bords des canaux d'Amsterdam, avec en tout vingt-cinq de ces bâtiments typiques pour Amsterdam.

El Pulitzer se encuentra en la famosa zona de canales de Amsterdam, y se compone de veinticinco típicas casas de canales.

All rooms display works of art by contemporary Dutch artists.

In sämtlichen Räumen finden sich Kunstwerke zeitgenössischer niederländischer Künstler.

La plupart des chambres abritent des œuvres d'art de peintres hollandais contemporains.

En todos los lugares del hotel puede encontrar obras de arte de artistas contemporáneos holandeses.

Amigo
Brussels, Belgium

Disagreements can sometimes have a touch of irony. The people of Brussels were amused by the fact that the reviled Spanish rulers translated the Flemish name of the building, which served as a prison in the 16th century, as "friend". And so, the name Amigo continues to adorn the imposing, red brick building with the Renaissance façade, only a few steps away from Brussels's famous Grand Place. Since its renovation in 2002 by the Rocco Forte Group, this distinguished luxury hotel no longer harbours any traces whatsoever of its former function. Designer Olga Polizzi has clearly left her mark, lending the 188-room building an air of elegant, contemporary understatement. Traditional Flemish elements, such as the authentic Brussels paving stone in the lobby or the valuable Gobelins on the walls, set a special tone.

Missverständnisse können manchmal eine feine Ironie haben. Den Brüsselern gefiel es, dass die ungeliebten spanischen Machthaber den flämischen Namen des Hauses, das im 16. Jahrhundert als Gefängnis diente, mit „Freund" übersetzten. Und so ist der Name Amigo dem stattlichen roten Backsteinhausbau mit der Renaissancefassade, nur wenige Schritte entfernt von Brüssels berühmtem Grand Place, erhalten geblieben. An seine frühere Bestimmung erinnert in dem distinguierten Luxushotel seit der aufwändigen Renovierung 2002 durch die Rocco-Forte-Gruppe rein gar nichts mehr. Unübersehbar ist die Handschrift der Designerin Olga Polizzi, die dem 188-Zimmer-Haus ein elegantes, zeitgemäßes Understatement verlieh. Traditionelle flämische Elemente wie der authentische Brüsseler Pflasterstein in der Lobby oder wertvolle Gobelins an den Wänden setzen besondere Akzente.

Parfois, les malentendus peuvent avoir une ironie raffinée. En tout cas, les Bruxellois eurent leur plaisir à ce que les dirigeants espagnols, qu'ils n'aimaient pas du tout, traduisirent le nom flamand de l'établissement, qui servait de prison au XVIe siècle, par « ami ». Et c'est ainsi que ce majestueux bâtiment en briques de terre cuite avec façade style Renaissance, qui est situé à quelques pas seulement de la célèbre Grand Place de Bruxelles, a conservé jusqu'à ce jour le nom « Amigo ». Cependant, depuis la rénovation extensive réalisée en 2002 par le groupe Rocco Forte, rien, absolument plus rien ne rappelle l'ancienne destination de cet hôtel de luxe distingué. La signature de la styliste Olga Polizzi, qui a conféré à cette résidence de 188 chambres une élégance et une modernité empreintes d'understatement. Des éléments flamands traditionnels comme le pavé mosaïque bruxellois authentique dans le lobby ou des Gobelins précieux sur les murs attireront aussi votre attention particulière.

Los malentendidos pueden ir aderezados a veces de una fina ironía. A los ciudadanos de Bruselas les gustó que los impopulares gobernantes españoles tradujeran como "amigo" el nombre flamenco de la casa, la cual sirvió como prisión en el siglo 16. Y así es como se ha mantenido el nombre de Amigo para el majestuoso edificio de ladrillo rojo con fachada renacentista, situado a sólo unos pasos de la famosa Grand Place de Bruselas. Desde la compleja renovación realizada en 2002 por el grupo Rocco Forte, nada recuerda a la anterior regulación del distinguido hotel de lujo. De valor incalculable es el manuscrito de la diseñadora Olga Polizzi, quien confirió un carácter elegante y discreto a la casa de 188 habitaciones. Algunos elementos flamencos tradicionales, como el empedrado auténtico de Bruselas en el vestíbulo o los valiosos tapices en las paredes, establecen acentos especiales.

Meeting point *for Brussels diplomats: lobby lounge and restaurant "Le Verlaine".*

Treffpunkt *für Brüsseler Diplomaten: Lobby Lounge und Restaurant „Le Verlaine".*

Point de rencontre *pour diplomates de Bruxelles . Lobby Lounge et Restaurant « Le Verlaine ».*

Centro de reunión *para diplomáticos de Bruselas: Lobby lounge y restaurante "Le Verlaine".*

Soft pastel tones characterize the warm, elegant style of the 188 rooms and suites.

Sanfte Pastelltöne bestimmen den warmen, eleganten Stil der 188 Zimmer und Suiten.

Le style chaleureux et élégant des 188 chambres et suites est déterminé par des tendres coloris pastel.

El estilo cálido y elegante de las 188 habitaciones y suites está marcado por tonos suaves pastel.

The Regent Schlosshotel Berlin

Berlin, Germany

A tiny pearl at the centre of the peaceful Grunewald: designed in 1914 as the private palace for the Walter Sigismund von Pannwitz family, the Schlosshotel mirrors the traditional character of the European grand hotels to this day. At the beginning of the 90s, fashion designer Karl Lagerfeld, lover of old estates, supervised the complete interior design. In co-operation with the architects Hasso von Werder and the London design agency Ezra Attia Design, Lagerfeld revitalised the gloss of an epoch passed. 42 rooms and 12 suites are located on three floors. Wellness and pleasure play a large role in this house from the Wilhelmina era. Thus the Chilean, Andrea Jiménez, treats her guests to aromatherapies and various facial and body treatments in her cosmetic studio. And the chef de cuisine Christian Lohse conjures up the finest gourmet specialities in the restaurant "Vivaldi".

Eine kleine Perle mitten im ruhigen Grunewald: 1914 als privates Palais der Familie Walter Sigismund von Pannwitz entworfen, spiegelt das Schlosshotel bis heute den traditionsreichen Charakter europäischer Grandhotels wider. Anfang der 90er Jahre übernahm Modeschöpfer Karl Lagerfeld als Liebhaber alter Herrschaftshäuser die Leitung der kompletten Inneneinrichtung. Zusammen mit dem Architekten Hasso von Werder und dem Londoner Designbüro Ezra Attia Design erweckte Lagerfeld hier den Glanz einer vergangenen Epoche zum Leben. 42 Zimmer und 12 Suiten verteilen sich auf drei Etagen. Wellness und Genuss spielen eine große Rolle in diesem Haus aus der wilhelminischen Ära. So kümmert sich die Chilenin Andrea Jiménez mit Aromatherapien und verschiedenen Gesichts- und Körperbehandlungen in ihrem Kosmetikstudio um die Gäste. Und der Chef de Cuisine Christian Lohse zaubert im Restaurant „Vivaldi" feinste Gourmet-Spezialitäten.

Une petite perle en plein centre du quartier calme de Grunewald : conçu en 1914 comme palais privé de la famille Walter Sigismund von Pannwitz, le Schlosshotel reflète aujourd'hui encore la richesse traditionnelle des Grand Hôtels européens. Au début des années 90, le grand couturier Karl Lagerfeld, amateur d'anciennes maisons seigneuriales, accepta de prendre en charge l'aménagement intérieur complet de l'établissement. En coopération avec l'architecte Hasso von Werder et Ezra Attia Design, bureau de design de Londres, Lagerfeld redonna à l'hôtel l'écat d'une époque ancienne. 42 chambres et 12 suites sont réparties sur trois étages. Le wellness et le délice jouent un rôle primordial dans cet établissement de l'ère wilhelmienne. Ainsi, la chilienne Andrea Jiménez offre dans son studio cosmétique des thérapies aromatiques et divers traitements du visage et du corps à ses hôtes. Et le chef de cuisine, Christian Lohse, crée comme par enchantement les spécialités gastronomiques les plus raffinées au restaurant « Vivaldi ».

Una pequeña perla situada en el centro del tranquilo bosque Grunewald: Diseñado en 1914 como palacio privado de la familia Walter Sigismund von Pannwitz, el castillo-hotel ha reflejado hasta hoy el carácter rico en tradición de los Grandhoteles europeos. A principios de los 90, el diseñador de moda Karl Lagerfeld, amante de viejas mansiones señoriales, se hizo cargo del completo diseño interior. En colaboración con el arquitecto Hasso von Werder y la oficina londinense de diseño Ezra Attia Design, Lagerfeld infundió vida al esplendor de épocas pasadas. 42 habitaciones y 12 suites se distribuyen por tres plantas. La relajación y el placer juegan un papel importante en esta casa de la época guillermina. Así, la chilena Andrea Jiménez se encarga de administrar a los clientes terapias aromáticas y diferentes tratamientos faciales y corporales en su estudio de cosmética, y el jefe de cocina Christian Lohse se saca de la "chistera" las más finas especialidades gastronómicas en el restaurante "Vivaldi".

New gloss on the former estate—Karl Lagerfeld shows that his talents do not only lie with garments. Here the fashion guru turns his attention to interior architecture.

Neuer Glanz der einstigen Pracht — Karl Lagerfeld beweist nicht nur Händchen für schöne Kleider. Hier wirkte der Modeschöpfer als Innenarchitekt.

Nouvel éclat de la magnificence d'antan — Karl Lagerfeld montre qu'il sait faire autre chose que de beaux habits. Le grand couturier s'est essayé ici comme architecte d'intérieur.

Nuevo esplendor de la pompa anterior; Karl Lagerfeld no sólo demuestra delicadeza para hermosos vestidos. El creador de moda desarrolla aquí sus habilidades como decorador de interiores.

Every room is furnished differently but nevertheless mirrors the elegance of the old estate.

Jedes Zimmer ist anders eingerichtet und spiegelt die Eleganz des alten Herrschaftspalais wider.

Chaque chambre est aménagée individuellement, mais reflète malgré tout l'élégance de l'ancien palais seigneurial.

Cada habitación tiene un diseño distinto, pero refleja sin embargo la elegancia del viejo palacio señorial.

Hotel zur Bleiche

Burg/Spreewald, Germany

An island of tranquillity, in the middle of the Spreewald forest. It takes just one hour by car from Berlin to reach this expansive hotel complex, offering utter enjoyment to convention guests and weekend holidaymakers alike. Especially the wellness offerings have been gradually expanded over time. A highlight is the separate, 2400 square metres bathhouse in the form of a barn. There, guests pamper themselves in the Jungbrunnen ("fountain of youth") Spa with massages or therapeutic baths, swim laps in the pool, or just relax in the fireplace room. The rooms of this country hotel are large and furnished in an appealing blend of modern and rustic elements.

Eine Insel der Ruhe, mitten im Spreewald. Nur eine Fahrtstunde ist es von Berlin hierher, in das großzügige Hotelareal, das Tagungsgästen wie Wochenend-Urlaubern vollendeten Genuss bietet. Schrittweise wurde in der vergangenen Zeit vor allem das Wellness-Angebot ausgebaut. Glanzstück ist ein separates, 2400 Quadratmeter großes Badehaus im Stil einer Scheune. Dort können sich die Gäste im Jungbrunnen Spa mit Massagen oder Heilwannenbädern verwöhnen lassen, im Pool ihre Bahnen schwimmen oder im Kaminzimmer ausspannen. Die Zimmer des Landhotels sind groß und in einer gelungenen modern-rustikalen Symbiose gestaltet.

Une oasis de paix, au milieu de la Spreewald. A une heure de trajet de Berlin seulement, le complexe spacieux de l'hôtel offre à des hôtes de séminaires comme à des vacanciers du week-end un plaisir inégalé. Pas à pas, l'offre wellness en premier lieu a été élargie. Le point phare est une maison de bains séparée d'une superficie de 2400 mètres carrés conçue sous la forme d'une grange. Là, les invités pourront se laisser cajoler dans le bain de jouvence Spa en recevant massages ou bains pleins de bienfaits, faire leurs brasses dans la piscine ou simplement se détendre devant la cheminée de leur chambre. Les chambres de l'hôtel campagnard sont spacieuses et conçues dans une symbiose moderne rustique très réussie.

Isla de tranquilidad en el centro del bosque Spreewald. La extensa área hotelera, que colma de placer a los clientes de conferencias y veraneantes de fin de semana, sólo se halla a una hora en coche de Berlín. Últimamente se ha ido ampliando poco a poco la oferta de relajación sobre todo. El centro de atención lo constituye un lugar de baños de 2400 metros cuadrados con estilo de un granero. Allí, en la "fuente de la eterna juventud" del balneario, los clientes pueden ser obsequiados con masajes o baños curativos en la bañera, nadar unos largos en la piscina o sólo relajarse en la habitación provista de chimenea. Las habitaciones del hotel rural son grandes y están equipadas en una acertada simbiosis de estilo moderno y rústico.

In a bath and wellness building, various beauty treatments and fitness programmes are offered.

In einem Bade- und Wellnesshaus werden verschiedene Beauty-Behandlungen und Fitness-Programme angeboten.

Différents soins de beauté et des programmes de fitness sont proposés à la Maison de bains et de wellness.

En una casa de baños y relajación se ofrecen diferentes tratamientos de belleza y programas de mantenimiento físico.

Country house style, designed in a modern way and enhanced by fine textiles and upholstery—that is the concept of the interior design.

Landhausstil, zeitgemäß umgesetzt und ergänzt durch feine Textilien und Polster – so sieht das Interieurkonzept aus.

Le concept de l'intérieur se décline comme suit : style campagnard, réalisé de manière intemporelle et complété par des textiles et des divans très raffinés.

Estilo de casa rural, renovada con carácter moderno y complementada con finos tejidos y tapices, así se manifiesta el concepto interior.

Grand Hotel Heiligendamm
Heiligendamm, Germany

Whatever Herzog Friedrich Franz I. von Mecklenburg-Schwerin did right in the year 1793, couldn't all be wrong two centuries later. This was the main idea behind the vision that the creators of the hotel had and in June 2003 they revived the magnificent hotel complex in the seaside resort of Mecklenburg bay. Six buildings are located over a surface area of 31,000 square metres allowing space for 118 rooms and 107 suites. The "white villas at the seaside" are framed by the sandy beach and park-like scenery consisting of beech tree forests and fields. The architect Robert A.M. Stern from New York and the Düsseldorf office HPP tended towards European-style furnishing as well as a slight Far Eastern touch. The rooms are furnished with light furniture combined with velvet and linen whereby the colors beige, rosé and green are dominant. The consistent orientation towards the sea is also retained in the Spa Center as well as on the golf grounds and stud farm.

Was Herzog Friedrich Franz I. von Mecklenburg-Schwerin im Jahre 1793 gut tat, kann zwei Jahrhunderte später nicht verkehrt sein. Dachten sich die Macher des Hotels und erweckten im Juni 2003 die prächtige Hotelanlage im Seebad in der Mecklenburgischen Bucht wieder zum Leben. Sechs Gebäude verteilen sich auf einer Fläche von 31.000 Quadratmetern und bieten Platz für 118 Zimmer und 107 Suiten. Die „weißen Villen am See" sind umrahmt von Sandstrand und einer parkartigen Kulisse aus Buchenwäldern und Wiesen. Der Architekt Robert A.M. Stern aus New York und das Düsseldorfer Büro HPP setzten auf europäisch geprägte Einrichtung und kleine Akzente aus Fernost. In den Zimmern finden sich helle Möbel kombiniert mit Samt und Leinen, wobei die Farben Beige, Rosé und Grün dominieren. Die konsequente Ausrichtung zum Meer bleibt auch im Spa-Center, auf dem Golfplatz und dem Reitgestüt erhalten.

Ce qui a fait du bien au Duc Frédéric François Ier de Mecklembourg-Schwerin en 1793 ne peut pas être absurde deux siècles plus tard. C'est bien ce qu'ont pensé les propriétaires de l'hôtel qui réanimèrent au mois de juin 2003 ce splendide complexe hôtelier à la station balnéaire de la Baie du Mecklembourg. Six bâtiments s'étendent sur une surface de 31 000 mètres carrés et offrent de la place pour 118 chambres et 107 suites. Les « villas blanches au bord du Lac » sont encadrées de sable de plage et d'une coulisse style parc de bois de hêtre et de pelouses. Les architectes, Robert A.M. Stern de New York et le bureau HPP de Düsseldorf, ont plutôt misé sur un aménagement empreint de style européen avec quelques accents d'Extrême-Orient. Dans les chambres, on retrouvera des meubles clairs combinés avec du velours et du lin, ce avec une nette prédominance des couleurs beige, rosé et vert. L'orientation conséquente vers la mer est aussi caractéristique du centre de spa, du terrain de golf et du complexe d'équitation.

La buena obra del duque Federico Francisco I de Mecklenburg-Schwerin realizada el año 1793 no puede ser errónea dos siglos después. Eso fue lo que pensaron los constructores del hotel, y en junio de 2003 volvieron a infundir vida a su magnífico recinto situado en la playa de la bahía de Mecklenburg. En una superficie de 31.000 metros cuadrados se distribuyen seis edificios que proporcionan espacio para 118 habitaciones y 107 suites. Las "blancas mansiones del lago" se hallan enmarcadas por playa con arena y un escenario de hayales y prados similar a un parque. Los arquitectos Robert A.M. Stern, de Nueva York, y el despacho de Düsseldorf HPP apostaron por un diseño con marcado estilo europeo y ligeros toques del lejano oriente. Las habitaciones brillantes se hallan provistas de muebles claros combinados con terciopelo y lino, predominando los colores beige, rosado y verde. El carácter consecuente del recinto situado en el mar se refleja también en el balneario, en el campo de golf y en el acaballadero.

The Estate combines the nostalgic charm of the White Town by the sea with the comfort of a luxury hotel with the highest of standards.

Das Anwesen verbindet einen nostalgischen Charme der Weißen Stadt am Meer mit dem Komfort eines Luxushotels für allerhöchste Ansprüche.

La propriété réunit un charme nostalgique de la Ville blanche sur la Mer au confort d'un hôtel de luxe qui satisfait aux exigences les plus rigoureuses.

La finca conjuga un encanto nostálgico de la ciudad blanca situada en el mar con la comodidad de un hotel de lujo de lo más exigente.

Light furniture with the colors beige, green and rosé arouse a feeling of noblesse.

Helle Möbel und die Farben Beige, Grün und Rosé erwecken ein Gefühl von Noblesse.

Les meubles clairs et les couleurs beige, vert et rosé donnent une impression de noblesse.

Los muebles claros y los colores beige, verde y rosado despiertan una sensación del nobleza.

Guests *can dine like royalty and enjoy after-dinner drinks on the column terrace with a view of the sea, in the spa house among hand-painted silk tapestries and chandeliers or in "Nelson Bar". Right: seating arrangement in one of the suites.*

Fürstlich *Speisen und Digéstifs genießen können die Gäste auf den Säulenterrassen mit Meerblick, im Kurhaus zwischen handbemalten Seidentapeten und Kronleuchtern oder in der „Nelson Bar". Rechts: Sitzgruppe in einer der Suiten.*

Les hôtes *peuvent prendre des repas majestueux et savourer des digéstifs sur les terrasses à colonnes avec vue sur la mer, dans l'établissement thermal, entouré de tapis en soie peints à la main et de lustres, ou dans le « Nelson Bar ». A droite : ensemble fauteuils et canapé dans l'une des suites.*

Los huéspedes *pueden degustar unos principescos manjares y digestivos enlas terrazas acolumnadas con vistas al mar, en el balneario entre tapices pintados a mano y candelabros o en el "Nelson Bar". A la derecha: grupo de asientos de una de las suits.*

Mandarin Oriental, Munich
Munich, Germany

Located between the Hofbräuhaus and Maximilianstraße this hotel transports a hint of luxury and elegance. When redesigning the former ball house the Californian architect Peter Remedios stated "The historic character of the Neo-Renaissance building has to be retained". Consistent with this idea, French and Italian marble, cherry-wood and ebony dominate the appearance of this noble domicile whether one is in one of the baths of the 53 rooms and 20 suites on the seven floors or on the curved steps on the way to Mark's Restaurant. However the guests do not only enjoy the view onto the marble stairs but they can also take pleasure in the fine dishes in one of Munich's five leading gourmet restaurants. In the L-shaped dining room creative delights are served with crystal and china porcelain.

Zwischen Hofbräuhaus und Maximilianstraße gelegen, versprüht dieses Hotel einen Hauch von Luxus und Eleganz. Das Credo des kalifornischen Architekten Peter Remedios lautete bei der Umgestaltung des ehemaligen Ballhauses: „Der historische Charakter des Neo-Renaissance-Baus muss bewahrt bleiben". So dominieren französischer und italienischer Marmor, Kirsch- und Ebenholz das Erscheinungsbild der Nobel-Herberge: ob in den Bädern der 53 Zimmer und 20 Suiten auf den sieben Etagen oder als geschwungene Treppe zum Mark's Restaurant. Die Gäste genießen dabei nicht nur den Anblick der Marmor-Stufen, sondern insbesondere die edlen Speisen eines der fünf führenden Gourmet-Restaurants Münchens. Im L-förmigen Speiseraum werden zwischen Tafelleinen, Kristall und China-Porzellan kreative Köstlichkeiten serviert.

Situé entre le Hofbräuhaus et la Maximilianstraße, cet hôtel dégage un soupçon de luxe et d'élégance. Le credo directeur de l'architecte californien Peter Remedios lors de la transformation de l'ancienne maison de bal était : « Le caractère historique de cette construction style néo-Renaissance doit absolument être préservé ». C'est ainsi que le marbre français et italien et le bois de cerisier et d'ébène dominent ici l'apparence de cet établissement de luxe, que ce soit dans les salles de bain des 53 chambres et 20 suites réparties sur sept étages que sous forme d'escaliers cintrés menant au Mark's Restaurant. Il va cependant sans dire que les hôtes ne jouissent ici pas seulement de la belle vue des marches en marbre, mais aussi – et tout particulièrement – des plats raffinés d'un des cinq meilleurs restaurants gastronomiques de Munich. Dans la salle à manger en forme de L, on vous servira des délices créatifs dans un décor de peintures sur voile, de cristal et de porcelaine de Chine.

Situado entre el Hofbräuhaus y la Maximilianstraße, este hotel desprende un hálito de lujo y elegancia. La divisa del arquitecto californiano Peter Remedios en la remodelación de la antigua casa de baile era: "Se ha de conservar el carácter histórico del edificio neorenacentista". De este modo, en el aspecto del noble hospedaje predomina el mármol francés e italiano y la madera de cerezo y ébano, bien sea en los baños de las 53 habitaciones y 20 suites distribuidas en siete plantas o en la escalera espiral que conduce al restaurante Mark's. Pero las clientes no sólo pueden disfrutar de la vista de los escalones de mármol, sino sobre todo de los nobles platos de uno de los cinco mejores restaurantes gastronómicos de Munich. En el comedor con forma de L se sirven creativas exquisiteces entre lienzos de lino, cristal y porcelana china.

Not only for gourmets—pure luxury reigns in this noble domicile situated between the Hofbräuhaus and Maximilianstraße.

Nicht nur für Gourmets – in der Nobelherberge zwischen Hofbräuhaus und Maximilianstraße herrscht Luxus pur.

Pas seulement pour les gourmets – Le luxe pur dans cet hôtel de luxe situé entre la Hofbräuhaus et la Maximilianstraße.

No sólo para gastrónomos; en el noble hospedaje situado entre el Hofbräuhaus y la Maximilianstraße reina el auténtico lujo.

The hustle and bustle of the town is completely forgotten in the swimming pool high above the roofs of Munich.

Das Treiben der Stadt ist im Swimmingpool hoch über den Dächern Münchens schnell vergessen.

L'agitation citadine s'oublie très rapidement lorsqu'on est à la piscine, bien haut sur les toits de Munich.

El ajetreo de la ciudad se olvida rápidamente en la piscina, situada divisando los tejados de Munich.

Mandarin Oriental, Munich *Munich, Germany* 57

La Réserve
Geneva, Switzerland

Ten minutes from the city centre and the airport, in a 4-hectare large park with lake access—an ideal location for a city resort. That is just what Michael Reybier thought when he purchased the property dating from the 60s and commissioned architect Patrice Reynaud and star interior decorator Jacques Garcia (Hotel Costes and L'hotel in Paris) with its complete renovation. The result is a central European oasis of relaxation with an African lodge character and gourmet Chinese cuisine, a fusion of styles with lots of creative surprises. One of the greatest is "le spa", a wellness facility with a 25-metre swimming pool, health restaurant, and a number of treatments that, if at all, can only be trumped by the wine list. In all, the hotel is right on the mark—if a bit on the modern side. Its international clientele as well as the Geneva elite have made it their new favourite place to be.

Zehn Minuten vom Stadtzentrum und vom Flughafen entfernt, in einem 4 Hektar großen Park mit Seeanschluß – ein idealer Platz also für ein Stadtresort. Dachte sich Michael Reybier, kaufte das Anwesen aus den 60er Jahren und beauftragte den Architekten Patrice Reynaud und Stareinrichter Jacques Garcia (Hotel Costes und L'hotel in Paris) mit der Komplettsanierung. Herausgekommen ist eine mitteleuropäische Entspannungsoase mit afrikanischem Lodgecharakter und chinesischer Gourmetküche, eine Fusion der Stile mit viel gestalterischer Überraschung. Zu den größten zählt „le spa", eine Wellnesslandschaft mit 25-Meter-Schwimmbad, Gesundheits-Restaurant und einer Vielzahl von Behandlungen, die allenfalls noch von der Weinkarte übertrumpft werden. Kurz: Ein Volltreffer — wenn auch ein wenig modisch — beim internationalen Publikum und der Genfer Nobelgesellschaft gilt die Adresse gleichermaßen als neuer Favorit.

Situé à dix minutes du centre-ville et de l'aéroport, dans un grand parc d'une superficie de 4 hectares offrant la possibilité de se rendre directement au bord du lac. Un lieu idéal pour un complexe hôtelier en ville, pensa Michael Reybier. Il acheta alors cette propriété érigée pendant les années 60 et chargea l'architecte Patrice Reynaud et le célèbre architecte d'intérieur Jacques Garcia (Hôtel Costes et L'hôtel à Paris) de l'assainir complètement. Une oasis de détente de l'Europe Centrale avec caractère de Lodge africain et une cuisine gastronomique chinoise avait vu le jour, une fusion des styles avec beaucoup de surprises du point de vue conceptionnel. « Le spa » compte parmi les plus grands, un paysage wellness avec une piscine de 25 mètres, un restaurant avec cuisine à orientation plutôt santé et un nombre important de soins. Tous sont néanmoins largement distancés par la carte des vins. En un mot : un tir au but bien placé – un tant soi peu à la mode – un public international. La haute société de Genève est unanime en ce que cette adresse est leur nouveau favori.

Situado a diez minutos del centro de la ciudad y del aeropuerto, en un parque de 4 hectáreas unido al lago. Un lugar ideal pues para un complejo en la ciudad. Esto fue lo que pensó Michael Reybier, quien compró la mansión de los años 60 y encargó su completa restauración al arquitecto Patrice Reynaud y al destacado diseñador Jacques Garcia (Hotel Costes y L'hotel in Paris). El resultado ha sido un oasis de relajación centroeuropeo con carácter de hospedaje africano y cocina gastronómica china, una fusión de estilos con muchas sorpresas creativas. Entre las mayores se cuenta "le spa" (el balneario), un paisaje de relajación con piscina de 25 metros, restaurante dietético y múltiples tratamientos que, en todos los casos, son incluso superadas por la carta de vinos. Resumiendo: Un acierto pleno, aunque con ciertos tintes de moda; el lugar se ha convertido al unísono en el nuevo favorito de los clientes internacionales y de la noble sociedad de Ginebra.

Not somewhere in Africa, but rather directly on Lake Geneva is the location of this luxurious, 100-room resort.

Nicht irgendwo in Afrika, sondern direkt am Genfer See liegt das luxuriöse 100-Zimmer Resort.

Ce complexe hôtelier luxurieux de 100 chambres n'est pas situé quelque part à l'Est d'Eden, mais directement aux bords du Lac Léman.

El lujoso complejo de 100 habitaciones no se encuentra en cualquier lugar de África, sino directamente en el lago Leman.

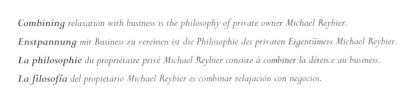

Combining relaxation with business is the philosophy of private owner Michael Reybier.

Enstpannung mit Business zu vereinen ist die Philosophie des privaten Eigentümers Michael Reybier.

La philosophie du propriétaire privé Michael Reybier consiste à combiner la détente au business.

La filosofía del propietario Michael Reybier es combinar relajación con negocios.

Especially *of note is its blend of interior decorating styles, combining the traditional with the modern from all continents.*

Bemerkenswert *ist die Stilmischung der Einrichtung aus Traditionellem und Modernen aus allen Kontinenten.*

On remarquera *bien le mélange de styles de l'aménagement intérieur alliant le traditionnel et le moderne de tous les continents.*

Es de destacar *la mezcla de estilos del complejo, con toques tradicionales y modernos de todos los continentes.*

Palace Luzern
Lucerne, Switzerland

Layer for layer, the Palace in Lucerne had to be freed of the renovation sins committed in past decades, before the 168-room grand hotel, situated on the lake promenade on Lake Lucerne, could fully unfold its belle-époque glory. In the lobby, which offers a breathtaking view of the lake and mountains, a drab wall-to-wall carpet was removed to reveal a gleaming, black-and-white marble floor, and wallpaper was taken down to expose valuable red scagliola columns. The "Jasper" Restaurant was newly opened, whose consistently modern interior design serves as a clever complement to the avant-garde Culture and Congress Centre, designed by star architect Jean Nouvel. Ever since the Congress Centre opened on the other side of the lake, it has been attracting big names in the classical music scene to Lucerne, who are especially fond of staying at the Palace.

Schicht um Schicht musste das Palace in Luzern von den Renovierungssünden der vergangenen Jahrzehnte befreit werden, bevor das an der Seepromenade des Vierwaldstättersees gelegene 168-Zimmer-Grandhotel seinen Belle-Epoque-Glanz wieder voll entfalten konnte. Unter einem faden Spannteppich in der Lobby mit ihrem traumschönen Blick auf See und Berge kam ein glänzender schwarz-weißer Marmorboden zu Tage, kostbare rote Stuckmarmorsäulen lagen unter Tapeten verborgen. Neu eröffnet wurde das Restaurant „Jasper", dessen konsequent modernes Interieurdesign ein kluges Pendant zu dem von Stararchitekt Jean Nouvel entworfenen avantgardistischen Kultur- und Kongresszentrum bildet, das seit seiner Eröffnung auf der anderen Seeseite die großen Stars der klassischen Musikszene nach Luzern zieht, die besonders gerne im Palace nächtigen.

Pas à pas, le Palace de Lucerne a dû être déblayé des diverses étapes des travaux des décennies précédentes, avant que ce grand hôtel de 168 chambres situé au bord de la promenade du lac des Quatre-Cantons ne révèle la splendeur de la Belle Epoque dans toute son ampleur. Le tapis fade tendu dans le lobby donnant sur la montagne et le lac s'est transformé en un sol en marbre noir et blanc rutilant. Les tapis ont donné naissance à des colonnes en marbre de stuc rouge enfouies d'une valeur inouïe. Le restaurant « Jasper » a été réouvert : son design intérieur résolument moderne offre un contraste intelligent au design avant-gardiste du Centre Culturel et de Congrès créé par le célèbre architecte Jean Nouvel. Depuis son ouverture à l'autre bout du lac, ce centre attire les plus grandes stars de la musique classique à Lucerne, et ces dernières résident volontiers au Palace.

El palacio de Lucerna tuvo que ser liberado piedra a piedra de los pecados renovadores de las últimas décadas, antes de que el Grandhotel de 168 habitaciones, situado en el paseo marítimo del lago de los cuatro cantones, pudiera volver a desplegar por completo su lustre de Belle-Epoque. Bajo un hilo de la moqueta del vestíbulo, desde el que puede disfrutarse de maravillosas vistas del lago y la montaña, salió a la luz un suelo de mármol blanco y negro brillante, y los tapices ocultaban rojas columnas valiosas en estuco de mármol. Se inauguró el nuevo restaurante "Jasper", cuyo moderno diseño interior consecuente sintoniza de forma ingeniosa con el vanguardista centro cultural y de congresos creado por el destacado arquitecto Jean Nouvel, centro que atrae a Lucerna a las grandes estrellas de la escena musical clásica desde su apertura al otro lado del lago, a quienes agrada pernoctar en el palacio.

Behind the 1906 art nouveau façade, one can experience the epitome of Swiss hospitality.

Hinter der Jugendstilfassade von 1906 lässt sich beste Schweizer Gastlichkeit erleben.

La façade art nouveau de 1906 reflète toute la tradition d'hospitalité de la Suisse.

Tras la fachada modernista de 1906 puede experimentarse auténtica hospitalidad suiza.

The latest renovation measures have restored belle-époque glory to the "Les Artistes" Restaurant and the lobby.

Mit der jüngsten Renovierung ist der Belle-Epoque-Glanz in das Restaurant „Les Artistes" und die Lobby wieder zurückgekehrt.

Les travaux les plus récents ont redonné au restaurant « Les Artistes » et au lobby toute la splendeur de la Belle Epoque.

Con las últimas renovaciones se ha recuperado el lustre de Belle-Epoque del restaurante "Les Artistes" y del vestíbulo.

The newly opened "Jasper" Restaurant, with its light, creative cuisine, sets a modern mood.

Einen modernen Akzent setzt das neue eröffnete Restaurant „Jasper" mit seiner leichten kreativen Küche.

Pour finir, le restaurant « Jasper » récemment ouvert parfait le tout et y donne une connotation moderne avec sa cuisine à tendance créative.

El nuevo restaurante "Jasper" está impregnado de un toque moderno con su cocina sutilmente creativa.

Hôtel Palafitte
Neuchâtel, Switzerland

If not for the fresh sea breeze in front and the exquisite vineyards in the back, you might think you were in the South Seas—because this five-star hotel is Europe's only "above-water hotel". The innovative pile design by Kurt Hofmann and his Atelier d'Architecture originated as the contribution of the Sandoz Foundation for the Swiss "Expo.02", intended as a luxurious, high-tech hotel for VIP's. Resonance for the temporary, 22-million frank building was overwhelming. It would be a great shame to have it open for just one summer, thought the operators, and so they endeavoured to make it permanent. Thus, the "jewel on the lake" was preserved for those looking for an unusual flair to their accommodations. Instead of opening room doors with a key, guests use their index fingers. Their biometric data are collected and entered into the system during check-in. Much like the house of the future, a hand-size plasma screen controls the lighting and blinds in the suites. Those who wish may descend directly to the lake from their bedroom terrace to have a healthy swim before indulging in a gourmet dinner in "Le Colvert".

Gäbe es nicht die frische Seebrise an der Front und die exquisiten Weinberge im Rücken könnte man sich auch in der Südsee wähnen, denn das Fünfsternehaus ist Europas einziges „Überwasser Hotel". Die innovativen Pfahlbauten von Kurt Hofmann und seinem Atelier d'Architecture waren der Beitrag der Sandoz-Stiftung zur Schweizer „Expo.02", für die Zeit der Ausstellung gedacht als luxuriöse High-Tech Unterkunft für VIP's. Das Echo auf das temporäre 22-Millionen Franken Objekt war überwältigend. Viel zu schade, um es nur einen Sommer lang zu öffnen, dachten sich die Betreiber und setzten es als Dauereinrichtung durch. So bleibt das „Juwel am See" allen erhalten, die das Ungewöhnliche suchen. Statt mit dem Schlüssel öffnet man die Zimmertüre mit seinem Zeigefinger. Seine biometrischen Daten gibt man beim Check-in ins System ein. Wie im Haus der Zukunft steuert ein handgroßer Plasmabildschirm die Beleuchtung und Jalousien in den Suiten. Wer möchte, kann von der Schlafzimmerterrasse direkt in den See hinabsteigen, um sich vor dem Gourmet-Dinner im „Le Colvert" noch einmal fit zu schwimmen.

S'il n'y avait pas la fraîche brise venant du lac arrivant en front d'hôtel et les vignes de tout premier cru en arrière-plan, l'on pourrait se croire quelque part en mer du Sud, car cet établissement cinq étoiles est le seul « hôtel sur eau » dans toute l'Europe. Les constructions sur pilotis innovatrices conçues par Kurt Hofmann et son atelier d'architecture étaient la contribution de la fondation Sandoz à « l'Expo.02 » en Suisse. A l'origine, cet hôtel a été conçu comme résidence high-tech luxurieuse pour recevoir les V.I.P. pendant la durée de l'exposition. L'écho enregistré concernant cet hôtel temporaire d'une valeur de 22 millions de francs suisses a été sans égal. Il aurait vraiment été bien dommage que cette aventure ne dure qu'un été ; c'est exactement ce que pensèrent les gérants : une demeure ouverte à plein temps venait ainsi de naître. Ce « bijou sur le lac » reste ainsi préservé pour tous les amoureux de l'inédit. La clé appartient définitivement à un passé bien révolu, on ouvre les portes des chambres avec l'index. On entre ses données biométriques dans le système au check-in. Comme dans une maison du futur, un écran plasma de la taille d'une main commande l'éclairage et les jalousies des suites. Quiconque le désire peut plonger directement dans le lac de la terrasse depuis sa chambre à coucher et se maintenir ainsi en forme avant le dîner gastronomique au « Le Colvert ».

Si no existiera la brisa fresca del lago delante y los exquisitos viñedos detrás podría uno creer que se encuentra en el Pacífico meridional, pues el alojamiento de cinco estrellas es el único "hotel sobre el agua" de Europa. Los innovadores palafitos de Kurt Hofmann y su estudio de arquitectura fueron la contribución de la fundación Sandoz a la "Expo.02", concebidos para el momento de la exposición como lujosos alojamientos de alta tecnología para VIP's. El eco de la construcción provisional de 22 millones de francos fue grandioso. "Una pena abrirlo sólo durante un verano", esto fue lo que pensaron los encargados y lo dejaron abierto permanentemente. Así pues, la "joya del lago" se conserva para todos aquellos buscan lo inusual. En lugar de utilizar una llave, las puertas de las habitaciones se abren con el dedo índice. Al registrarse se introducen sus datos biométricos en el sistema. Como en la casa del futuro, una pantalla de plasma del tamaño de una mano controla la iluminación y las persianas en las suites. Quien así lo desee puede bajar desde la terraza del dormitorio directamente al lago para ponerse nuevamente en forma nadando antes de la cena gastronómica en "Le Colvert".

Transparent architecture and an even balance of warm materials and decent, light colors lend the 40 pavilions their cosy, relaxed atmosphere.

Transparente Architektur und eine ausgewogene Mischung aus warmen Materialien und dezent hellen Farbtönen sorgen in den 40 Pavillons für eine wohnlich-entspannte Atmosphäre.

Une architecture transparente et un mélange équilibré de matériaux chauds et de tons clairs décents confèrent à la résidence une atmosphère détendue dans les 40 pavillons.

La transparente arquitectura y una mezcla equilibrada de materiales cálidos y discretos tonos de colores brillantes se encargan de proporcionar una atmósfera relajante y acogedora en los 40 pabellones.

 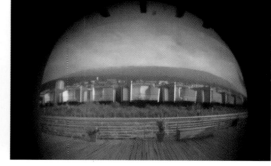

The main building houses the reception desk, lobby, fireplace bar and gourmet restaurant "Le Colvert". The high-tech suites are accessible via wooden gangways.

Im Hauptgebäude sind Empfang, Lobby, Kaminbar und das Gourmetrestaurant „Le Colvert". Über Holzstege gelangt man zu den High-Tech Suiten.

Le bâtiment principal abrite la réception, le lobby, le bar-cheminée et le restaurant gastronomique « Le Colvert ». Les suites high-tech sont accessibles empruntant les pilotis de bois.

En el edificio principal se encuentra la recepción, el vestíbulo, el bar con chimenea y el restaurante gastronómico "Le Colvert". A las suites altamente tecnológicas se accede a través de pasarelas de madera.

Hôtel des Trois Couronnes

Vevey, Switzerland

Prominent guests are by no means rare in this hotel, originating from the age of historicism—whether they are stars and starlets from the world of the media, or statesmen of rank and reputation. This may have a great deal to do with the hotel's proximity to Geneva, with the fascinating view of Lake Geneva and the towering Alps framing Mont Blanc beyond it, or perhaps the impressive promenade terrace in the front yard. Ultimately, however, its greatest draw is the hotel's top level of style and service, which boast over a hundred years of tradition, and whose charms even fascinated Thomas Mann. The lakeside restaurant alone, with its light and elegant radiance, is an enticement itself. In the hallways and open balcony corridors, marble columns are resplendent in magnificent historicism. In contrast, the rooms and suites are an appealing mixture of traditional and modern elements. They combine stylish living with a youthful taste in art and interior decorating. Accordingly, the hotel houses a new, very minimalist wellness centre. Its highlight is the fitness room: a chill-out room with parquet, chandeliers and an open marble fireplace.

Prominente sind in diesem Hotel, das aus der Zeit des Historismus stammt, keine Seltenheit; seien es Stars und Sternchen aus der Welt der Medien oder Staatsmänner von Rang und Namen. Das mag viel mit der Nähe zu Genf zu tun haben, mit dem faszinierenden Blick auf den Genfer See und die dahinter aufragenden Alpen um den Mont Blanc. Oder auch mit der imposanten Promenadenterrasse vor dem Haus. Am Ende aber überzeugt wohl am allermeisten der internationale Top Level in Stil und Service des Hotels, das auf eine mehr als hundertjährige Geschichte zurückblickt und dessen Charme schon Thomas Mann erlag. Bereits das lichte und Eleganz ausstrahlende Restaurant an der Seeseite zieht eine eigene Aufmerksamkeit auf sich. In den Gängen und offenen Balkonfluren prangen Marmorsäulen in wunderbarem Historismus. Die Räume und Suiten präsentieren sich dagegen in einer sympathischen Mischung aus traditionell und modern. Sie verbinden stilvolles Wohnen mit jungem Geschmack in Kunst und Interieur. Entsprechend gibt sich das neue, sehr minimalistisch gehaltene Wellnesszentrum des Hauses. Der Clou ist der Fitness-Raum: Chill-Out-Zone mit Parkett, Kronleuchter und Marmorkamin.

Les célébrités ne sont pas du tout rares dans cet hôtel de l'époque de l'historisme, qu'il s'agisse de stars et starlettes du monde des médias ou d'hommes d'états de haut rang et de renommée. Peut-être que cela s'explique par la proximité de Genève, avec la vue fascinante sur le Lac Léman et les Alpes, entourant le Mont Blanc, qui s'étendent derrière. Ou bien par la terrasse imposante de la promenade devant l'établissement. Néanmoins, en fin de compte, c'est plutôt et surtout le Top Level international caractérisant le style et le service de l'hôtel, qui a une histoire de plus de cents ans et fascina jadis Thomas Mann, qui vous convaincra. Le restaurant élégant et inondé de lumière, tourné vers la rive du lac, attire déjà tout seul les regards. Dans les corridors et balcons ouverts, des colonnes en marbre témoignent d'un historisme magnifique. Les pièces et suites se présentent par contre avec un mélange sympathique de traditionnel et de moderne. Elles combinent, en ce qui concerne l'art et leur aménagement intérieur, l'ameublement de style avec le goût jeune. C'est ce qui caractérise aussi le nouveau centre de wellness, très minimaliste, de l'établissement. Le clou, c'est la salle de fitness et de musculation, une zone de relaxation avec parquet, lustres et cheminée en marbre !

No es raro encontrar famosos en este hotel que proviene de la época del historicismo, bien sean estrellas y aspirantes a ello del mundo de los medios u hombres de estado con rango y nombre. Esto puede asociarse con las proximidades de Ginebra, con la fascinante vista del lago Leman y los Alpes que se elevan detrás en torno al Mont Blanc, o también con la imponente terraza del paseo situado delante del hotel. Sin embargo, lo que al final convence en mayor medida es probablemente un estilo y servicio del hotel que destaca por su nivel internacional, que se retrotrae a una historia de más de cien años y ante cuyos encantos sucumbió Thomas Mann. El restaurante en la parte de la orilla llama ya la atención por la luz y elegancia que irradia. En los corredores y pasillos de balcones abiertos resplandecen columnas de mármol cargadas de un historicismo maravilloso. Las habitaciones y suites se hallan provistas, por el contrario, de una simpática mezcla de tradicionalismo y modernidad. Combinan un aspecto lleno de estilo con el gusto jovial por el arte y los interiores. Análogamente aparece el nuevo centro de relajación de la casa, conservado con un carácter bastante minimalista. El plato fuerte lo constituye la sala de mantenimiento físico: Zona relajante con parqué, lámparas de corona y chimenea de mármol.

Captivating is the view of Lake Geneva—whether from the promenade terrace or the wrought-iron balconies.

Einnehmend der Blick auf den Genfer See – ob von der Promenadenterrasse oder den schmiedeeisernen Balkonen aus.

La vue sur le Lac Léman est captivante – que ce soit depuis la terrasse de la promenade ou depuis les balcons en fer forgé.

La vista del lago Leman resulta seductora, bien sea desde la terraza del paseo o desde los balcones de hierro forjado.

Corridors *and hallways still radiate the glow of days gone by. In the rooms, the spirit of the modern age has taken hold.*

Gänge *und Flure verströmen noch den Glanz vergangener Zeiten. In den Räumen hat der Esprit der Moderne Einzug gehalten.*

Les corridors *et couloirs sont encore témoins de l'éclat des temps passés. Dans les pièces, l'esprit du moderne est dorénavant bien présent.*

Los corredores *y pasillos aún desprenden el fulgor de épocas pasadas. En las habitaciones ha hecho acto de presencia el espíritu de la modernidad.*

In the suites, one can dine privately, framed by bookcases. Spaciousness that is also reflected by the hotel pool.

In den Suiten lässt es sich privat dinieren, eingerahmt von einer Schrankwand mit Büchern. Großzügigkeit, die das hauseigene Schwimmbad ebenfalls vermittelt.

Dans les suites, on peut très confortablement dîner en privé, encadré par des éléments muraux garnis de livres. Cette générosité, ce caractère spacieux se retrouvent également dans la piscine de l'hôtel.

En las suites pueden llevarse a cabo cenas privadas, enmarcadas por un armario de pared con libros. Se observa una prodigalidad que también transmite la piscina propia del hotel.

Hotel Imperial
Vienna, Austria

Emperor Franz Josef himself opened this upper-class hotel on 28 April 1873 on the occasion of the World Fair in Vienna. It has clearly always been a place where the rich and powerful have met. Today, too, all official state guests of Austria stay in this luxury hotel. In 1994, the readers of "Condé Nast Traveler Magazine" voted this residence on the Wiener Ringstraße as the best hotel on the planet. With 138 rooms and 32 suites, it offers enough space to relax in comfort after a hard day of negotiating. Valuable antiques and a spectacular painting collection lend the house an air of Vienna of the 19th century. The hotel's butler service is probably unique: The butlers iron the newspapers so that guests will not dirty their hands with the black ink.

Kaiser Franz Josef höchstpersönlich eröffnete am 28. April 1873 das Nobelhotel zum Anlass der Weltausstellung in Wien. Klar, dass es immer ein Ort gewesen ist, wo sich Reiche und Mächtige trafen. Auch heute noch residieren alle Staatsgäste Österreichs in der Luxusherberge. 1994 wählten die Leser von „Condé Nast Traveler Magazine", die Residenz an der Wiener Ringstraße zum besten Hotel rund um den Globus. 138 Zimmer und 32 Suiten bieten genügend Platz, um sich nach anstrengenden Verhandlungen gemütlich zurückzulehnen. Wertvolle Antiquitäten und eine üppige Gemäldesammlung verleihen dem Haus ein Ambiente vom Wien des 19. Jahrhunderts. Und einmalig ist wohl der Butlerservice des Hauses: Da bügeln die Butler die Zeitungen, damit sich der Gast nicht mit der Druckerschwärze der Blätter beschmutzt.

L'Empereur Francois-Joseph Ier d'Autriche en personne a inauguré ce palais royal le 28 avril 1873 à l'occasion de l'exposition mondiale qui se tenait à Vienne. Il est clair que cet hôtel était prédestiné pour devenir le rendez-vous de prédilection des riches et des puissants de ce monde. Aujourd'hui encore, tous les invités du gouvernement autrichien se rencontrent dans cette résidence de luxe. En 1994, les lecteurs du « Condé Nast Traveler Magazine » ont choisi à l'unanimité la résidence de la Wiener Ringstraße comme étant le meilleur hôtel du globe. 138 chambres et 32 suites offrent suffisamment d'espace pour se détendre en toute tranquillité après des débats ardus. Des antiquités d'une valeur inestimable et une collection de tableaux non négligeable confèrent à cette résidence une ambiance de Vienne au XIXe siècle. Le service du personnel de l'hôtel n'a pas son pareil dans le monde. Les employés repassent même les journaux afin que les hôtes ne se salissent pas au contact de l'encre des journaux !

El noble hotel fue abierto personalmente por el emperador Francisco José el 28 de abril de 1873 con motivo de la exposición universal de Viena. El mismo fue siempre un lugar de encuentro para gente rica y poderosa. Los invitados de estado de Austria siguen hospedándose en la actualidad en el parador de lujo. En 1994, los lectores de "Condé Nast Traveler Magazine" eligieron a la residencia de la Ringstraße de Viena como el mejor hotel del mundo. 138 habitaciones y 32 suites ofrecen suficiente espacio para recostarse cómodamente tras negociaciones estresantes. Valiosas antigüedades y una fastuosa colección de cuadros confieren al hotel un ambiente vienés del siglo 19. También resulta singular el servicio de mayordomo de la casa: Los mayordomos planchan aquí los periódicos para que el cliente no se manche con la tinta de imprenta de las hojas.

Royal is an apt description for this upper-class hotel on the Wiener Ringstraße. Emperor Franz Josef himself gazed down at guests on a daily basis.

Königlich geht es in diesem Nobelhotel an der Wiener Ringstraße zu. Nicht umsonst blickt Kaiser Franz Josef täglich auf die Gäste herunter.

Simplement royal, est le seul qualificatif convenable de l'atmosphère qui existe dans ce noble hôtel de la Wiener Ringstraße. Ce n'est pas un hasard si l'Empereur François-Joseph Ier d'Autriche y veille tous les jours, présent en toile de fond, au bien-être de ses hôtes.

La vida se desarrolla con tintes de realeza en este noble hotel de la Ringstraße de Viena. No en vano, el emperador Francisco José observa diariamente desde arriba a los clientes.

Chandeliers, stucco ceilings, antiques and paintings. Royal grandeur with a touch of Franz Josef and Sissi emanates from every corner.

Kronleuchter, Stuckdecken, Antiquitäten und Gemälde. Königlicher Prunk mit Franz Josef und Sissi Flair strahlt aus allen Winkeln.

Lustres, plafonds en stuc, antiquités et tableaux caractérisent cet hôtel de luxe. Un apparat royal avec en filigrane le flair de l'Empereur François-Joseph et de Sissi est omniprésent.

Lámparas de corona, techos de estuco, antigüedades y cuadros. Todas las esquinas irradian pompa real con estilo de Francisco José y Sissi.

Plaza Athénée

Paris, France

The popular Parisian interior designer Patrick Jourin redesigned the "Bar du Plaza". Ever since, it has been a must for Parisian society and a crowd-puller for the legendary hotel. This deluxe establishment, founded in 1911, is situated on Avenue Montaigne, surrounded by trendy boutiques, fine restaurants and businesses. Despite comprehensive renovation, one can still perceive the radiance of days gone by in the Plaza Athénée. Furniture and accessories in the hotel are reminiscent of the classical French style. A few of the 40-square-metre deluxe suites offer an idyllic view of the garden.

Der angesagte Pariser Designer Patrick Jourin gestaltete die „Bar du Plaza" neu. Seitdem ist sie eine Muss-Adresse für die Pariser Gesellschaft und ein Aushängeschild des legendären Hotels. Die 1911 in Betrieb genommene Luxusherberge liegt an der Avenue Montaigne, umgeben von Trendboutiquen, feinen Restaurants und Geschäftshäusern. Trotz einer umfangreichen Sanierung ist im Plaza Athénée der Glanz vergangener Zeiten zu spüren. Möbel und Accessoires im Hotel greifen den klassischen, französischen Stil auf. Einige der 40 Quadratmeter großen Deluxe-Zimmer bieten einen idyllischen Blick in den Garten.

Patrick Jourin, renommé styliste d'intérieur parisien, a remodelé le « Bar du Plaza ». Depuis lors, cette adresse est un must pour la société parisienne et sert d'image de marque pour le légendaire hôtel. Cette résidence de luxe, qui a ouvert ses portes en 1911, se trouve à l'Avenue Montaigne, entourée de boutiques au top de la tendance, de nobles restaurants et d'immeubles de bureaux. Malgré les travaux d'assainissement de très grande envergure qui y ont été effectués, on ressent à la Plaza Athénée la splendeur du passé. Les meubles et accessoires à l'intérieur de l'hôtel reprennent le style classique français. Certaines des grandes chambres « Deluxe », qui ont 40 mètres carrés, offrent une vue idyllique sur le jardin.

El famoso diseñador parisino de interiores Patrick Jourin efectuó la reestructuración del "Bar du Plaza". El mismo constituye desde entonces un lugar de destino para la sociedad parisina y un estandarte del legendario hotel. El hospedaje de lujo inaugurado en 1911 se encuentra en la avenida Montaigne, rodeado de boutiques de moda, finos restaurantes y tiendas comerciales. A pesar de haber sufrido una amplia restauración, en el Plaza Athénée puede percibirse el brillo de épocas pasadas. Los muebles y accesorios del hotel se asocian al estilo clásico francés. Algunas de las habitaciones de lujo de 40 metros cuadrados ofrecen una visión idílica del jardín.

The hotel offers enough places to spend a couple of relaxing hours. In the summer, guests often sit in the courtyard.

Das Hotel bietet genügend Plätze für schöne Stunden. Im Sommer sitzen die Gäste gerne im Innenhof.

L'hôtel offre suffisamment de places pour passer des heures agréables. En été, les hôtes se prélassent avec plaisir sur les bancs de la cour intérieure.

El hotel ofrece suficiente espacio para horas agradables. En verano suele apetecer a los clientes sentarse en el patio interior.

The lobby and bar of the hotel are spacious rooms with class and elegance. Tradition is preserved everywhere.

Lobby und Bar des Hotels sind großzügige Räume mit Klasse und Eleganz. Die Tradition wird überall bewahrt.

Le lobby et le bar de l'hôtel, des grands espaces avec beaucoup de classe et d'élégance. La tradition est respectée partout.

El vestíbulo y el bar del hotel son espacios amplios con clase y elegancia. La tradición se conserva por doquier.

All rooms have been modernized and updated with regard to technical amenities. Thus, business travellers will find optimal conditions when they come to Paris.

Alle Zimmer wurden modernisiert und technisch aufgerüstet. So finden Geschäftsreisende jetzt optimale Bedingungen vor, wenn sie in Paris sind.

Toutes les chambres ont été modernisées et dotées d'un équipement technique amélioré. Les V.R.P. seront maintenant hébergés dans des conditions optimales lorsqu'ils sont à Paris.

Todas las habitaciones fueron modernizadas y equipadas técnicamente. De este modo, los viajeros de negocios encuentran ahora condiciones óptimas cuando están en París.

Le Dokhan's
Paris, France

The elegance and charm of an aristocratic Parisian private home is radiated by Dokhan's, renovated in 1999 to become a small, intimate luxury hotel. Situated somewhat hidden in the well-to-do 16th arrondissement between Trocadéro and the Arc de Triomphe, this 45-room establishment is considered one of the best kept secrets of the city on the Seine. Decorating the hotel was the job of French star interior decorator Frédéric Méchiche's dreams. He was granted carte blanche, and able to draw on abundant resources. Méchiche did not create a boutique hotel, but rather a haute-couture house, with the entire interior created as a unique work: Rugs were woven according to 18th century themes, old parquet floors were laid in artistic patterns, the walls were either hand-painted or covered in heavy fabrics—and an original Louis Vuitton wardrobe trunk even serves as a lift.

Eleganz und Charme eines noblen Pariser Privathauses kultiviert das 1999 zum kleinen, intimen Luxushotel umgebaute Dokhan's. Ein wenig versteckt im feinen 16. Arrondissement zwischen Trocadéro und Arc de Thriomphe gelegen, gilt das 45-Zimmer-Haus als eines der bestgehüteten Geheimnisse der Seine Metropole. Für den französischen Starinnenarchitekten Frédéric Méchiche war die Einrichtung ein Traumjob. Er hatte carte blanche, konnte aus dem Vollen schöpfen. Méchiche kreierte kein Boutiquehotel, sondern ein Haute-Couture-Haus, denn das gesamte Interieur wurde als Unikat gefertigt: Teppiche nach Motiven aus dem 18. Jahrhundert gewebt, altes Parkett in kunstvollen Mustern verlegt, die Wände von Hand bemalt oder mit schweren Stoffen bespannt – und als Aufzug dient ein original Louis Vuitton Schrankkoffer.

L'élégance et le charme d'une demeure parisienne privée sont cultivés dans le petit hôtel intime de luxe transformé en 1999 par Dokhan's. Un peu caché, dans le quartier chic du XVIe arrondissement, entre le Trocadéro et l'Arc de Triomphe, cette maison aux 45 chambres est considéré comme l'un des secrets les mieux gardés de la métropole au bord de la Seine. Pour Frédéric Méchiche, architecte d'intérieur français renommé, l'aménagement du bâtiment a correspondu à un travail de rêve. Il avait carte blanche et a donc pu puiser largement dans les ressources. Méchiche n'a pas créé un hôtel boutique, mais une maison de Haute Couture, car tout l'intérieur a été fabriqué comme objet unique : les tapis tissés selon des motifs du XVIIIe siècle, le parquet posé en motifs savants, les murs peints à la main ou revêtus de tentures lourdes, et en guise d'ascenseur, un original d'une malle-armoire de Louis Vuitton.

Transformado en 1999 en un hotel de lujo pequeño e íntimo, Dokhan's cultiva la elegancia y el encanto de una noble casa privada parisina. Situada algo oculta en el fino distrito 16, entre Trocadéro y Arc de Thriomphe, la casa de 45 habitaciones está considerada como uno de los secretos mejor guardados de la metrópoli del Sena. Su construcción fue un trabajo de ensueño para el destacado arquitecto francés de interiores Frédéric Méchiche. El mismo tenía carta blanca para desplegar todo su ingenio. Méchiche no creó un hotel-boutique, sino una casa de "alta costura", pues todo su interior fue acabado como algo único: Alfombras tejidas con motivos del siglo 18, viejos parqués colocados con muestras artísticas, las paredes pintadas a mano o revestidas con telas pesadas, y como ascensor sirve un original baúl de Louis Vuitton.

The typical Parisian façade in Baron Haussmann style. From the Suite Eiffel, one has a breathtaking view of the Eiffel Tower.

Die typische Pariser Fassade im Stil von Baron Haussmann. Von der Suite Eiffel genießt man einen traumhaften Blick auf den Eiffelturm.

Façade typiquement parisienne selon le style du Baron Haussmann. De la suite Eiffel, on jouit d'une vue splendide sur la Tour Eiffel.

Su fachada es tipicamente parisina, con estilo del barón Haussmann. Desde la suite Eiffel puede disfrutarse de una vista de ensueño de la torre Eiffel.

Neoclassical *mélange: the two salons with detailed stucco and precious wooden panelling from the 18th century.*

Neoklassizistische *Mélange: die beiden Salons mit aufwändigen Stuckaturen und der kostbaren Holzvertäfelung aus dem 18. Jahrhundert.*

Mélange *de néoclassicismes: deux salons aux grands ornements en stucs et boiseries de grande valeur datant du XVIIIe siècle.*

Mezcla *neoclásica: Los dos salones, con complejas estructuras y un valioso revestimiento de madera del siglo 18.*

Under the roof: the Ming Suite, in blue and white, with its Chinese vases.

Unterm Dach: die blau-weiß gehaltene Ming-Suite mit ihren chinesischen Vasen.

Sous le toit: la suite Ming conservée dans les tons de bleu et blanc avec ses vases chinois.

Bajo el techo: La suite Ming, conservada en azul y blanco con sus jarrones chinos.

Château de Massillan

Uchaux, France

Behind a façade dominated by mighty towers hides a small, very contemporary hotel, whose simply-designed reception area could just as easily be found in London. This four-star hotel, situated 30 kilometres north of Avignon, houses just 20 rooms and suites. Three friends converted it from a 16th century, provincial hunting lodge. Traces of the spirit of its previous owner, Diane de Poitiers, the mistress of Henry II, who was beautiful and, for the times, incredibly emancipated, can still be felt. Two of the new owners run the design company Babylon in London, from where the modern lamps originate. These lamps combine with French antiques from the 18th and 19th century. The third owner is chef Marc Koenemund of Hamburg, whose cooking skills are highly acclaimed, enticing visitors to indulge in culinary delight.

Hinter einer Fassade, dominiert von mächtigen Türmen, verbirgt sich ein kleines, sehr zeitgemäßes Hotel, dessen schlicht gestaltete Rezeption sich so ähnlich auch in London finden könnte. Gerade mal 20 Zimmer und Suiten hat das Viersternehotel, 30 Kilometer nördlich von Avignon, das drei Freunde in einem provenzalischen Jagdschloss aus dem 16. Jahrhundert einrichteten und das noch immer den Geist seiner früheren Besitzerin, Diane de Poitiers, der Maitresse Heinrichs II., atmet, die bildschön und für ihre Zeit unglaublich emanzipiert war. Zwei der neuen Besitzer betreiben die Designfirma Babylon in London, von dort kommen die modernen Leuchten, die kombiniert wurden mit französischen Antiquitäten aus dem 18. und 19. Jahrhundert. Dritter im Bunde ist Küchenchef Marc Koenemund aus Hamburg, dessen Kochkünste hochgelobt werden und manchen Gast zu einem kulinarischen Abstecher verleiten.

Derrière une façade dominée par d'imposantes tours, se cache un petit hôtel tout à fait au goût du jour, dont la réception très simplement décorée pourrait également se trouver dans un hôtel londonnien. Il n'y a que 20 chambres et suites dans cet hôtel quatre étoiles situé à 30 kilomètres au nord d'Avignon, que trois amis ont arrangé dans un château provencal datant du XVIe siècle, où l'on pratiquait la chasse ; et ceci tout en conservant l'esprit de la propriétaire d'antan, Diane de Poitiers, maîtresse d'Henri II, une femme superbe et incroyablement émancipée pour l'époque. Deux des nouveaux propriétaires dirigent l'entreprise de design Babylon à Londres. C'est de là que proviennent les luminaires modernes qui ont été combinés aux antiquités françaises du XVIIIe et XIXe siècle. Le troisième allié est le chef cuisinier, Marc Koenemund de Hambourg, dont l'art culinaire est très prisé et qui conduit les visiteurs à faire un détour pour goûter à ces délicatesses du palais.

Detrás de una fachada y dominado por imponentes torres se oculta un pequeño y moderno hotel cuya recepción tiene una disposición similar a la que podría encontrar en Londres. Este hotel de cuatro estrellas sólo cuenta con 20 habitaciones y suites, está situado 30 kilometres al norte de Avignon y fue convertido por tres amigos en un pabellón de caza provenzal del siglo 16 que aún conserva el espíritu de su antigua propietaria, Diane de Poitiers, concubina de Heinrich II, una mujer bellísima e increíblemente emancipada para su época. Dos de los nuevos propietarios gestionan la empresa de diseño Babylon de Londres, y de allí provienen las modernas lámparas que fueron combinadas con las antigüedades francesas de los siglos 18 y 19. El tercero en discordia es el jefe de cocina Marc Koenemund de Hamburgo, ensalzado por sus artes profesionales, que han inducido a algún que otro cliente a efectuar una incursión culinaria.

The 20 rooms and suites are kept in a unique mix of old and new styles. Framed, hand-painted wallpaper serves as a substitute for pictures.

Die 20 Zimmer und Suiten sind in einem eigenwilligen Stilmix aus Alt und Neu gehalten, eine gerahmte handgemalte Tapete dient als Bildersatz.

Les 20 chambres et suites sont un mélange voulu de styles anciens et modernes, une tapisserie dessinée à la main, encadrée, fait usage de tableau.

Las 20 habitaciones y suites se hallan diseñadas con una mezcla arbitraria de estilo antiguo y moderno; un tapiz enmarcado y pintado a mano sirve como sustitución de cuadros.

The green courtyard, enclosed by the three wings of the hunting lodge, and the winter garden, with its filigree chairs, are perfect for relaxing.

Wunderbar entspannen lässt es sich im grünen Innenhof, den drei Flügel des Jagdschlosses umschließen, oder im Wintergarten mit seinen filigranen Sesseln.

On peut parfaitement se relaxer dans la cour intérieure de verdure, entourée de trois ailes du château de chasse, ou encore dans le jardin d'hiver doté de sièges filigranes.

En el patio interior con zonas verdes puede uno relajarse maravillosamente, el cual se halla rodeado por tres alas del pabellón de caza, o en el invernadero con sus sillones de filigrane.

Attractive contrast: The solid-colored modern wool material on the upholstered furniture comes from Scotland.

Reizvoller Kontrast: Die unifarbenen modernen Wollstoffe der Sitzmöbel stammen aus Schottland.

Les tissus de laine unis, modernes des sièges proviennent d'Ecosse et produisent un contraste tout à fait charmant.

Encantador contraste: Los modernos tejidos de lana monocolor de los asientos provienen de Escocia.

Villa d'Este
Como, Italy

As early as 1568, master builder Pellegrino Pellegrini started construction of a cardinal residence directly on picturesque Lake Como. Three centuries later, the Queen's Pavilion was added, and in 1873, both villas were united and the Grand Hotel "Villa d'Este" was born. Today, guests will find 161 rooms and suites in which brocade and linen are the dominating materials. Some rooms have a terrace or balcony. A walk around the 25-acre private park surrounding the villas is always worthwhile. The fitness and wellness options span from windsurfing to water-skiing to relaxing in a Turkish bath. And after the rigors of the day, guests can enjoy Italian haute cuisine in the "Veranda" Restaurant or Japanese specialities in "Kisho".

Schon 1568 macht sich Baumeister Pellegrino Pellegrini direkt am herrlichen Comersee an den Bau einer Kardinalsresidenz. Drei Jahrhunderte später kommt der Queen's Pavillon dazu, und 1873 werden die beiden Villen schließlich vereint und das Grand Hotel „Villa d'Este" eröffnet seine Pforten. Heute präsentieren sich den Gästen 161 Zimmer und Suiten, in denen die Materialien Brokat und Leinen dominieren. Manche Zimmer sind mit Terrasse oder Balkon ausgestattet, und ein Spaziergang im zehn Hektar großen Privatpark rund um die Villen lohnt sich immer. Die Fitness- und Wellness-Angebotspalette reicht vom Windsurfen über Wasserski bis hin zur Entspannung im türkischen Bad. Und nach den Anstrengungen des Tages genießen die Gäste die italienische Haute Cuisine im Restaurant „Veranda" oder japanische Köstlichkeiten im „Kisho".

Déjà en 1568, le bâtisseur Pellegrino Pellegrini entrepend la construction d'une résidence de cardinaux située directement au bord du lac de Côme. Trois siècles plus tard, cette résidence s'enrichit du Queen's Pavillon, et en 1873 les deux villas finissent par être réunies : le grand hôtel « Villa d'Este » est né. Aujourd'hui, 161 chambres et suites attendent leurs invités. Les matériaux brocart et lin prédominent. Certaines chambres ont une terrasse ou un balcon, et une promenade dans le parc privé d'une superficie de 10 hectares autour des villas vaut toujours un détour. La palette de fitness et de wellness va du surf au ski nautique jusqu'à la détente dans les hammams. Et après tous les efforts fournis pendant la journée, les invités peuvent savourer la haute cuisine italienne au restaurant « Veranda » ou les spécialités japonaises au « Kisho ».

En la época tan lejana de 1568, el arquitecto Pellegrino Pellegrini se dispuso a construir una residencia de cardenales justo frente al maravilloso lago Como. Tres siglos más tarde se añadió el Queen's Pavillon, y en 1873 se unieron finalmente las dos mansiones y abrió sus puertas el Grand Hotel "Villa d'Este". Los clientes pueden disponer hoy de 161 habitaciones y suites, donde predominan materiales de brocado y lino. Algunas habitaciones se hallan provistas de terraza o balcón, y siempre merece la pena dar un paseo alrededor de las mansiones por el gran parque privado de diez hectáreas. La oferta de mantenimiento físico y tratamientos medicinales se extiende desde deportes de surf hasta relajacion en baños turcos, pasando por esquí acuático. Y tras las estresantes actividades cotidianas, los clientes pueden disfrutar de la alta cocina italiana en el restaurante "Veranda", o de exquisiteces japonesas en "Kisho".

Two villas join to make one hotel—whether the cardinal's residence or the Queen's Pavilion: both take guests back to eras gone by.

Zwei Villen vereinen sich zu einem Hotel – ob Kardinalsresidenz oder Queen's Pavillon: beiden entführen die Gäste in vergangene Zeiten.

Deux villas regroupées dans un seul et même hôtel. Qu'il s'agisse de la résidence des cardinaux ou du Queen's Pavillon, ces deux résidences entraînent les invités dans les époques passées.

Hotel compuesto por dos mansiones, la residencia de cardenales y el Queen's Pavillon: Ambos transportan a los clientes a épocas pasadas.

Brocade and linen dominate in the 161 rooms and suites. The large windows offer a view of the private park.

Brokat und Leinen dominieren in den 161 Zimmern und Suiten. Die großen Fenster bieten einen Blick in den Privatpark.

Le brocard et le lin prédominent dans les 161 chambres et suites. Les grandes fenêtres offrent une vue imprenable sur le parc privé.

En las 161 habitaciones y suites predomina el brocado y el lino. Las grandes ventanas ofrecen una vista del parque privado.

Viewing *Lake Como directly from the swimming pool or enjoying massages and Turkish baths in the Spa Centre—the hotel accentuates fitness and relaxation.*

Vom Swimmingpool *direkt auf den Comersee schauen oder im Spa-Center Massagen und türkische Bäder genießen – das Hotel setzt auf Fitness und Entspannung.*

Depuis *la piscine, les hôtes peuvent bénéficier de la vue directe sur le lac de Côme, ou bien ils apprécieront les massages dans le centre de Spa et les hammams – l'hôtel mise sur le fitness et la détente pure.*

Desde *la piscina puede divisarse directamente el lago Como o disfrutarse de masajes y baños turcos en el balneario, el hotel apuesta por el mantenimiento físico y la relajación.*

Villa San Michele
Florence, Italy

Monastery-like seclusion of an especially luxurious sort: High above the Arno Valley, in the hills of Fiesole, Franciscan monks established a monastery in the early 15th century. Since 1982, the retreat, from whose restaurant loggia one has a magnificent view of the historical city centre of Florence, has belonged to the Orient Express Hotel Group, which renovated the establishment in cooperation with the Instituto delle belle Arti of Florence. The dignified monastery atmosphere has been largely preserved in the rooms—the dark, terracotta floors and wooden ceiling beams uncovered, and the entryway, with its columns, attributed to Michelangelo, renovated in the most meticulous manner. Since the mid-nineties, thirteen new junior suites have been built. From their private gardens, guests can enjoy a wide panorama of Florence, much like the view from the heated outdoor pool and its sun terrace.

Klösterliche Abgeschiedenheit in einer besonders luxuriösen Variante: Hoch über dem Arno-Tal, in den Hügeln Fiesoles, gründeten Franziskanermönche Anfang des 15. Jahrhunderts ein Kloster. Seit 1982 gehört das Refugium, von dessen Restaurant-Loggia man einen traumhaften Blick auf die Altstadt von Florenz genießt, der Orient-Express Hotel-Gruppe, die es in enger Zusammenarbeit mit dem Instituto delle belle Arti von Florenz restaurierte. Das erhabene klösterliche Ambiente der Räume wurde bewahrt, die dunklen Terrakottaböden und Holzdeckenbalken freigelegt, der Eingangsbereich mit seinen Säulen, der Michelangelo zugeschrieben wird, aufs sorgsamste wiederhergestellt. Seit Mitte der neunziger Jahre wurden dreizehn Juniorsuiten neu gebaut. Von ihren Privatgärten genießt man einen weiten Blick auf Florenz, genauso wie vom beheizten Außenpool und der Sonnenterrasse.

Un cloître dans un lieu reculé, en version particulièrement luxueuse : bien au-dessus de la vallée de l'Arno, dans les collines de Fiesole, des moines franciscains ont fondé un cloître au début du XVe siècle. Dans ce coin retiré, on jouit sur la loggia du restaurant d'une splendide vue sur la vieille ville de Florence. Il appartient depuis 1982 au groupe hôtelier Orient-Express qui l'a restauré en collaboration avec l'Instituto delle belle Arti de Florence. L'ambiance de cloître d'antan a été conservée dans les différentes pièces, les sols terracotta sombres et les poutres de bois aux plafonds ont été mis en valeur et l'entrée avec des colonnes, dédiée à Michel-Ange, a été on ne peut plus soigneusement restaurée. Depuis le milieu des années quatre-vingt-dix, treize suites junior ont été construites. Dans les jardins privés, mais aussi de la piscine extérieure chauffée sur la terrasse au soleil, on a une ample vue sur Florence.

Aislamiento conventual en una variante especialmente lujosa: A principios del siglo 15 unos monjes franciscanos fundaron un convento en las colinas Fiesoles, en lo alto del valle del Arno. El refugio pertenece desde 1982 al grupo hotelero Orient-Express, que lo restauró en estrecha colaboración con el Instituto delle belle Arti de Florencia, y desde la logia del restaurante puede disfrutarse de una vista fantástica de la parte vieja de la ciudad. Se conservó el sublime ambiente conventual de las habitaciones, se descubrió el suelo oscuro de terracota y las vigas del techo de madera y se restauró con el máximo esmero la zona de entrada y sus columnas, atribuidas a Miguel Ángel. Desde mediados de los noventa se construyeron trece suites juveniles nuevas. Desde sus jardines privados puede disfrutarse de una vista lejana de Florencia, como también desde la piscina externa con calefacción y su terraza para tomar el sol.

Five-star luxury behind monastery walls. In the early 15th century, the Villa San Michele was built high over Florence.

Fünf-Sterne-Luxus hinter klösterlichen Mauern. Anfang des 15. Jahrhunderts wurde die Villa San Michele hoch über Florenz erbaut.

Un luxe cinq étoiles se cache derrière les murs d'un cloître. Au début du XVe siècle, la Villa San Michele a été construite sur une hauteur autour de Florence.

Lujo de cinco estrellas tras los muros del convento. A principios del siglo 15 se construyó la mansión San Michele en la parte alta de Florencia.

The design of the 21 rooms and 24 suites, with their dark furniture and lavish fabrics, reflects the majestic character of the building.

Die Einrichtung der 21 Zimmer und 24 Suiten reflektiert mit ihren dunklen Möbeln und aufwändigen Stoffen den erhabenen Charakter des Gebäudes.

L'agencement des 21 chambres et 24 suites reflète bien le caractère d'origine du bâtiment grâce aux meubles sombres et aux tissus raffinés.

Con sus muebles oscuros y lujosos tejidos, el diseño de las 21 habitaciones y 24 suites refleja el carácter sublime del edificio.

110   Villa San Michele *Florence, Italy*

Villa San Michele *Florence, Italy* 111

Villa Feltrinelli
Gargnano, Italy

Guests of the Villa Feltrinelli know what it's like to experience luxury beyond the usual standard of five-star hotels. On the refined west bank of Lake Garda, in the middle of a sprawling park with a stock of precious, centuries-old trees, the American Bob Burns—founder of the Regent Group—has created a refuge of superlatives. More than 80 personnel serve guests accommodated in just 21 rooms and suites: the "smallest Grandhotel in the world". The Liberty Style private villa of the legendary Italian publishing family Feltrinelli, built in 1892, has been restored with strict adherence to laws relating to the protection of historical monuments. No expense has been spared. With obsessive meticulousness the glorious opulence of the historic rooms, as well as the valuable furnishings within, have been recreated.

Jenseits aller Sterne ist der Luxus, der Gäste in der Villa Feltrinelli erwartet. Am feinen Westufer des Gardasees inmitten eines weitläufigen Parks mit jahrhundertealtem kostbaren Baumbestand gelegen, hat der Amerikaner Bob Burns, der frühere Besitzer der Regent-Gruppe, ein Refugium der Superlative geschaffen. Von mehr als 80 Angestellten werden die Gäste der nur 21 Zimmer und Suiten im „kleinsten Grandhotel der Welt" umsorgt. Unter strengen Auflagen des Denkmalschutzes wurde die 1892 im Libertystil erbaute Privatvilla der legendären italienischen Verlegerfamilie Feltrinelli mit einem ungeheuren finanziellen Aufwand restauriert. Mit geradezu obsessiver Akribie hat man die prachtvolle Opulenz der historischen Räume, samt den kostbaren Originalmöbeln, wieder hergestellt.

Le luxe qui attend les visiteurs de la Villa Feltrinelli est au delà de toute catégorie étoiles. Sur la rive ouest du lac de Garde, au milieu d'un immense parc aux superbes arbres centenaires, l'Américain Bob Burns, ancien propriétaire du groupe Regent, a créé un refuge des superlatifs. Les visiteurs des quelques 21 chambres et suites du « plus petit Grandhôtel du monde » sont choyés par 80 employés. La villa privée de la légendaire famille italienne d'éditeurs, Feltrinelli, construite en 1892 dans le style « liberty » a été restaurée dans le stricte respect de la protection des monuments historiques, à des coûts exhorbitants. L'opulence somptueuse des pièces historiques a été restituée ainsi que les meubles d'origine d'une grande valeur, le tout dans un esprit méticuleux presque obsessionnel.

El lujo que espera a los clientes de la villa Feltrinelli está más allá de cualquier estrella. Situada en medio de un extenso parque con rico arbolado de siglos de antigüedad en la fina ribera occidental del lago Garda, el americano Bob Burns, anterior propietario del grupo Regent, creó un refugio de carácter superlativo. Los clientes de las escasas 21 habitaciones y suites del "Grandhotel más pequeño del mundo" son atendidos por más de 80 empleados. Bajo estrictas condiciones del patrimonio artístico nacional, la villa privada construida en 1892, en estilo liberty, por la legendaria familia italiana de editores Feltrinelli fue restaurada con una enorme inversión financiera. La suntuosa opulencia de las habitaciones históricas, incluidos los valiosos muebles originales, fue restablecida con un rigor casi obsesivo.

The entrance area reminds one of a Venetian Palazzo, with a view through to Lake Garda.

An einen venezianischen Palazzo erinnert der Eingangsbereich, der einen Durchblick bis auf den Gardasee gewährt.

L'entrée avec vue assurée sur le lac de Garde, fait penser à un palais vénicien.

La zona de entrada trae a la memoria palacios venecianos, y permite obtener una vista del lago Garda.

With an obsession for detail and a feeling for the subtle use of color, the historical splendor of the building has been brought back to life.

Detailbesessen und mit einem feinen Gespür für Farbnuancen wurde die prunkvolle historische Bausubstanz wieder sichtbar gemacht.

Les murs ont retrouvé leur somptuosité passée grâce à des travaux hantés par le détail et par un sens rafiné des nuances de couleurs.

Con una obsesión por los detalles y un fino olfato por los matices de color, reverdeció de nuevo el fastuoso e histórico espíritu del edificio.

116 Villa Feltrinelli *Gargnano, Italy*

An invitation to afternoon tea in the opulent salon of an upper-class family.

Der opulente Salon einer großbürgerlichen Familie lädt zum Nachmittagstee ein.

Le salon opulent d'une grande famille bourgeoise invite à la cérémonie du thé dans le courant de l'après-midi.

El opulento salón de una familia de la alta burguesía invita al té de sobremesa.

Bright whites contrast with the darkness of brightly polished wood, to lend the suites a contemporary elegance.

Weiß verleiht der Suite mit ihren dunklen, auf Hochglanz polierten Hölzern eine zeitgemäße Eleganz.

Le blanc combiné aux boiseries sombres, brillantes de polissure, donne à la suite une élégance adaptée au temps.

Con sus maderas oscuras pulidas en intenso brillo, el color blanco confiere a la habitación una elegancia actual.

Four Seasons Hotel Milano
Milan, Italy

Once a monastery, now a luxury hotel not far from Via Montenapoleone, the classiest shopping mile in Milan. This meticulously renovated building, with its frescoes and pictures, is the epitome of Italian art and design. The deluxe hotel in Italy's fashion capital houses 118 rooms and suites, and also welcomes children. Large French windows in the suites offer a magnificent view of the private gardens. Those not having access to that view can simply stroll along the columns around the courtyard. In "Il Teatro" Restaurant, guests enjoy excellent northern Italian cuisine, and in "La Veranda", Sergio Mei's team serves delicious Mediterranean specialties. To burn off those pounds again, hotel guests can head to the hotel's own fitness centre.

Einst ein Kloster, heute eine Luxusherberge nicht weit von der Via Montenapoleone, der edelsten Shoppingmeile Mailands entfernt. Dieses aufwändig restaurierte Haus liefert mit seinen Fresken und Bildern ein Zeugnis italienischer Kunst und des Designs. 118 Zimmer und Suiten finden sich in der Luxusherberge der Modestadt, auch Kinder sind in diesem Haus willkommen. Große französische Fenster der Suiten bieten einen herrlichen Blick auf den Privatgarten. Wer diesen nicht genießen kann, schlendert einfach entlang der Säulen rund um den Innenhof. Im Restaurant „Il Teatro" schlemmen die Gäste exzellente norditalienische Speisen und im „La Veranda" serviert das Team um Sergio Mei leckere mediterrane Küche. Um die Pfunde wieder abzutrainieren, nehmen die Hotelbesucher einfach den Weg in das hauseigene Fitness-Center.

Jadis un cloître, aujourd'hui une résidence luxueuse située à deux pas de la Via Montenapoleone, la zone de shopping la plus huppée de Milan. Magnifiquement restaurée, cette demeure avec ses fresques et ses peintures célèbre l'art et le design italiens dans leurs plus pures traditions. Dans cette résidence de luxe de la capitale de la mode par excellence qui abrite 118 chambres et suites, les enfants non plus ne sont pas laissés pour compte. Les grandes fenêtres à la française offrent une vue de tout premier plan sur le jardin privé. Tout hôte ne pouvant pas bénéficier de cette vue imprenable pourra flâner autour des colonnes bordant la cour intérieure. Dans le restaurant « Il Teatro », les hôtes dégusteront d'excellentes créations de la cuisine de l'Italie du Nord. Une cuisine méditerranée délicieuse vous attend à « La Veranda », servie par le chef cuisinier Sergio Mei et son équipe. Tout est prévu pour faire disparaître les kilos superflus, l'hôtel est équipé de son propre centre de musculation et de fitness.

Antiguamente era un convento y actualmente es un parador de lujo cercano a la Vía Montenapoleone, la más zona de compras más noble de Milán. Restaurada por todo lo alto, los frescos y cuadros de esta casa son testimonio del arte y diseño italiano. Este parador de lujo de la ciudad de la moda, donde igualmente son bien recibidos los niños, cuenta con 118 habitaciones y suites. Las grandes ventanas francesas de las suites ofrecen una vista maravillosa del jardín privado. Quien no pueda disfrutar del mismo, podrá caminar tranquilamente a lo largo de las columnas que rodean el patio interior. En el restaurante "Il Teatro" los clientes pueden saborear excelentes platos del norte de Italia, y en "La Veranda", el personal en torno a Sergio Mei sirve exquisita cocina mediterránea. Para perder los kilos ganados, los visitantes del hotel pueden hacer uso del propio centro de mantenimiento físico.

In the 15th century, praying monks once wandered through the cloister; today, hotel guests stroll here.

Im 15. Jahrhundert wanderten einst betende Mönche durch den Kreuzgang, heute lädt er Hotelgäste zum Flanieren ein.

Au XVe siècle, des moines en prière se promenaient dans le cloître. Aujourd'hui, il invite les hôtes à y flâner tout simplement.

En el siglo 15 deambulaban los monjes por el claustro dedicados a la oración; hoy invita el hotel a sus clientes a pasear por el mismo.

The interior of the luxury hotel also reflects the former monastery atmosphere. Bright colors provide refreshing accents.

Auch im Innern des Luxushotels spiegelt sich die einstige Klosteratmosphäre wider. Bunte Farben sorgen für erfrischende Akzente.

L'atmosphère de jadis se reflète également à l'intérieur de cet hôtel de luxe. Les couleurs colorées confèrent à cet hôtel une connotation très rafraîchissante.

En el interior del hotel de lujo también se refleja la atmósfera conventual del pasado. Diversos colores le impregnan toques refrescantes.

Whether round arches in the foyer or stucco ceilings in the rooms—this elegant hotel houses evidence of past eras.

Ob Rundbögen in der Eingangshalle oder Stuckdecken in den Zimmern – die Nobelherberge liefert ein Zeugnis vergangener Epochen.

Qu'il s'agisse des arcades ou des plafonds en stuc dans les chambres, cette résidence de luxe témoigne d'époques prestigieuses du passé.

Bien sean los arcos de medio punto en el hall de entrada o los techos de estuco en las habitaciones, el albergue noble es un testimonio de épocas pasadas.

Brufani Palace
Perugia, Italy

The Palace, conceived as a grand hotel in 1884 by Giacomo Brufani, crowns the viewing platform of Perugia's promenade street. Not only does the red and brown façade bear witness to the generosity of Italian building design; the interior, as well, greets guests with the same degree of grandezza formerly reserved for the noble class and other high-ranking individuals. The atrium lobby, with its lead-glazed ceiling, a cosy bistro, a classy restaurant, historical banquet hall, room with a fireplace, suites and guest rooms: all rooms are abundantly decorated, opulently furnished, yet without a trace of stuffiness. Everything functions smoothly, and with a serenity that makes a stay in such a noble establishment pleasant even for "normal" people. Thus, it would be quite unspectacular if you sipped your aperitif in the bar next to Brufani enthusiasts such as Queen Elizabeth or Prince Albert of Monaco.

Wie gemalt thront das 1884 von Giacomo Brufani als Grandhotel konzipierte Palais an der Aussichtsplattform von Perugias Flaniermeile. Nicht nur die rotbraune Fassade bestimmt die Großzügigkeit italienischer Baukunst, auch im Innern wird der Gast von jener Grandezza empfangen, die früher dem Adel und anderen hochrangigen Persönlichkeiten vorbehalten war. Atrium-Lobby mit bleiverglaster Decke, gemütliches Bistro, Nobelrestaurant, historischer Festsaal, Kaminzimmer, Suiten und Gästezimmer: alle Räume sind reichlich verziert, üppig ausgestattet aber nie überladen oder aufdringlich und schon gar nicht steif. Alles „funktioniert" mit jener Unaufgeregtheit, die den Aufenthalt in einem Traditionshaus auch für Normalbürger angenehm machen. So wäre es heute wohl auch ganz unspektakulär, wenn die Brufani-Anhänger Queen Elizabeth oder Prinz Albert von Monaco neben einem an der Bar ihren Aperitif genießen würden.

Beau comme une image, ce palais conçu comme grand hôtel par Giacomo Brufani en 1884 trône sur la plate-forme panoramique du quartier de promenade de Pérouse. Le caractère spacieux de l'architecture italienne s'exprime pleinement sur la façade couleur rouge brun, comme à bien d'autres endroits ; à l'intérieur également, c'est la grandeur réservée jadis à la noblesse et autres personnalités de haut rang de ce monde qui attend le visiteur. Le lobby-atrium avec plafond résille, le bistro intime, le restaurant de luxe, la salle des fêtes historique, la chambre à cheminée, les suites et les chambres d'hôtes, toutes les pièces sont richement ornées, avec un aménagement luxurieux, sans pourtant jamais être surchargées ou envahissantes et encore moins guindées. Tout « fonctionne » bien avec ce laisser-faire qui rend le séjour dans un établissement riche en tradition agréable aussi pour le commun des mortels. De nos jours, cela ne surprendrait certainement même plus que la Reine Elisabeth ou le Prince Albert de Monaco, adeptes du Brufani Palace, prennent un apéritif au bar à côté de soi.

Como si estuviera pintado reina el palacio concebido como Grandhotel por Giacomo Brufani en 1884 en la vista panorámica de la zona peatonal de Perugia. No sólo la fachada roja-marrón determina la generosidad del arte arquitectónico italiano; el cliente también es recibido en el interior por aquella grandeza que en el pasado estaba reservada para la nobleza y otras personalidades de postín. Vestíbulo-atrio con techo emplomado, bistro acogedor, noble restaurante, sala de fiestas histórica, habitación con chimenea, suites y salas de invitados: todas las zonas se hallan profusamente adornadas, suntuosamente equipadas pero sin sobrecargarse o resultar molestas en ningún caso, y menos aún mostrando rigidez. Todo "funciona" con esa tranquilidad que también hace agradable la estancia a ciudadanos normales en una casa tradicional. De este modo, a nadie sorprendería hoy encontrarse con la reina Isabel de Inglaterra o el príncipe Alberto de Mónaco, simpatizantes de Brufani, disfrutando de su aperitivo en el bar.

Stylish elegance is united with a relaxed atmosphere at Brufani Palace. A highlight is the swimming pool (with a sauna, fitness area and steam bath) resting on its Etruscan foundations on the sublevel.

Stilvolle Eleganz vereint das Brufani Palace mit lockerer Atmosphäre. Ein Highlight ist das Schwimmbad (mit Sauna, Fitness und Dampfbad) auf etruskischen Fundamenten im Untergeschoss.

L'élégance stylée s'allie à une atmosphère détendue au Brufani Palace. Un des clous du complexe est la piscine (avec sauna, fitness et bain de vapeur). Elle est bâtie sur des fondations étrusques à l'étage inférieur.

El palacio Brufani combina elegancia cargada de estilo y atmósfera relajada. Un punto principal lo constituye la piscina (con sauna, centro de mantenimiento físico y baño de vapor) construida sobre cimientos etruscos en la planta baja.

Impressive panoramic views of Perugia and Umbria are available in most of the rooms, but especially from the restaurant on the roof terrace.

Beeindruckende Panoramaaussichten über Perugia und Umbrien bieten die meisten Zimmer, vor allem aber das Restaurant auf der Dachterrasse.

Une impressionnante vue panoramique sur Pérouse et l'Ombrie, c'est ce que vous offrent la plupart des chambres et, avant tout, le restaurant sur la toiture-terrasse.

La mayoría de las habitaciones ofrecen impresionantes vistas panorámicas de Perugia y Umbría, pero sobre todo el restaurante de la terraza.

Brufani Palace *Perugia, Italy* 129

Each of the 94 rooms and suites is decorated in a different, mostly brilliant, color and equipped with cushy furniture.

Alle 94 Gästeräume und Suiten sind in verschiedenen, meist kräftigen Farben gestaltet und mit plüschigem Mobiliar ausgestattet.

Chacune des 94 chambres d'hôtes et les suites sont aménagées individuellement avec des couleurs le plus souvent vives et équipées d'un mobilier pelucheux.

Cada una de las 94 habitaciones y suites se hallan concebidas en distintos colores, generalmente fuertes, y equipadas con muebles afelpados.

Hotel de Russie
Rome, Italy

Casual elegance rather than superficial grandeur: in the middle of Rome's lively Centro Storico, between the Piazza del Popolo and the Spanish Steps, designer Olga Polizzi has created a veritable city oasis. The flagship hotel of the Rocco Forte Group oozes relaxed contemporary chic, neatly integrating a mix of styles from the 1930s and 40s with the modern works of art. The terracotta colored town houses which make up the 129 room hotel—including 24 suites—encircle a dream-like Mediterranean terraced courtyard. Rome's most elegant citizens come to relax with an aperitif after a long day of shopping in the designer stores nearby.

Lässige Eleganz statt vordergründigem Prunk: Mitten im quirligen Centro Storico Roms, an der Piazza del Popolo, nur wenige Schritte entfernt von der Spanischen Treppe hat die Designerin Olga Polizzi eine ganz besondere Stadt-Oase kreiert. Sie kultivierte im Flagschiffhaus der Rocco-Forte-Gruppe einen entspannten zeitgemäßen Chic, dessen Stilmix Elemente aus den 30er und 40er Jahren enthält, die gekonnt kombiniert werden mit zeitgenössischen Kunstwerken. Die terrakottafarbenen Stadthäuser mit ihren 129 Gästezimmern, davon 24 Suiten, gruppieren sich um einen traumschönen mediterranen Terrasseninnenhof, wohin elegante Römer und Römerinnen gerne zum Aperitif kommen – nach höchst aufwändigen Shopping-Touren in den umliegenden Designerläden.

Une élégance détendue sans luxe ostentatoire : Au beau milieu du Centro Storico de Rome, à la Piazza del Popolo, à quelques pas de l'escalier espagnol, la créatrice de design Olga Polizzi, est à l'origine d'une Oasis toute particulière au milieu de la ville. Dans la maison du vaisseau amiral du groupe Rocco-Forte, elle a su cultiver un chic contemporain détendu, dont le style comprend des éléments des années 30 et 40 qu'elle a combinés, avec un savoir-faire certain, à des œuvres d'art contemporaines. Les maisons de la ville dans les tons de terracotta présentent 129 chambres dont 24 suites et se regroupent en une merveilleuse cour intérieure sous forme de terrasse au style méditerrannéen, où les élégants otochtones aiment venir prendre l'apéritif après avoir fait leurs achats de première classe dans les magasins design des alentours.

Elegancia desenfadada en lugar de ostensible suntuosidad: A mitad del alegre Centro Storico de Roma, en la plaza del Popolo, a pocos pasos sólo de la escalera española, la diseñadora Olga Polizzi ha creado un oasis muy especial en la ciudad. En la casa del buque insignia del grupo Rocco Forte cultivó un lugar glamouroso, moderno y relajado cuya mezcla de estilos contiene elementos de los años 30 y 40 combinados hábilmente con obras de arte contemporáneas. Las casas adosadas con colores cocidos y sus 129 habitaciones, 24 de ellas suites, se agrupan alrededor de un patio interior con terraza de estilo mediterráneo y de ensueño, adonde suelen acudir los romanos elegantes para tomar el aperitivo, tras extenuantes recorridos de compras por las tiendas de diseñadores de las inmediaciones.

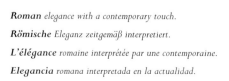

Roman elegance with a contemporary touch.
Römische Eleganz zeitgemäß interpretiert.
L'élégance romaine interprétée par une contemporaine.
Elegancia romana interpretada en la actualidad.

Terracotta colored tones highlight the Mediterranean atmosphere.

Terrakottatöne unterstreichen die mediterrane Atmosphäre.

Les teinte de terracotta soulignent l'ambiance méditerrannéenne.

Atmósfera mediterránea acentuada por matices cocidos.

Clear lines and simple decorative effects reflect the ambience of the rooms. The mosaic bathrooms provide a touch of old Rome.

Klare Linien und wenige ausgesuchte Dekorationsstücke bestimmen das Ambiente der Zimmer, die Mosaikbäder zitieren römische Vorbilder.

Des lignes claires et peu de détails décoratifs, c'est ce qui caractérise l'atmosphère des chambres. Les salles de bains à mosaïques sont à l'exemple du style romain.

El ambiente de las habitaciones se caracteriza por líneas diáfanas y algunos elementos decorativos selectos; los baños con mosaicos hacen referencia a modelos romanos.

Bauer Venezia
Venice, Italy

Royal families, actors and the international jet set keep coming back to this opulent retreat, situated directly on the Canale Grande. Its exterior is a rather hard to pinpoint ensemble of former Palazzo and contemporary construction. This Grand Hotel, established in 1880, is the best address in Venice for slumber as well as fine dining, as its regulars can tell you. Yet perhaps it is also the almost excessive furnishings—a successful blend of styles, from rococo to art deco—that so fascinate guests and flaneurs alike. If you are lucky enough to stay here, you can experience Venice's savoir vivre right from the terraces: gondolas, the stillness between the houses, elegant people and a great deal of history. Breakfast on the roof terrace is a must. An unparalleled sight: the panorama of the city on the lagoon.

Königsfamilien, Schauspieler und der internationale Jetset kommen immer wieder gerne in das direkt am Canale Grande gelegene Refugium. Ein von außen nur schwer zu erfassendes Ensemble aus ehemaligem Palazzo und Neubau. Das 1880 gegründete Grandhotel ist nach Meinung der Stammgäste die erste Adresse zum Schlafen und Schlemmen in Venedig. Vielleicht ist es aber auch die fast verschwenderische Ausstattung – eine gelungene Stilmischung, von Rokoko bis Art Déco – der die Gäste und Flaneure begeistert. Wer das Glück hat, hier zu nächtigen, erlebt von den Terrassen aus das Savoir-vivre von Venedig: Gondeln, die Stille zwischen den Häusern, elegante Menschen und viel Geschichte. Nicht auslassen sollte man ein Frühstück auf der Dachterrasse. Unvergleichlich: Das Panorama über die Lagunenstadt.

Familles royales, acteurs et les membres du jet-set international visitent fréquemment avec beaucoup de plaisir ce refuge situé directement au bord du Canale Grande. Une symbiose, difficile à appréhender de l'extérieur, d'ancien palazzo et de nouvelle construction. Ce Grand Hôtel, fondé en 1880, est, à en croire ses fidèles hôtes, le meilleur endroit qu'offre Venise pour dormir et se régaler. Peut-être aussi est-ce l'aménagement presque prodigue – un mix réussi de styles, du Rococo à l'Art Déco – qui enthousiasme tant les hôtes et les flâneurs. Quiconque a la chance de passer la nuit ici pourra, depuis les terrasses, voir ce que signifie savoir-vivre à Venise : gondoles, le calme entre les maisons, des femmes et hommes élégants et une riche histoire. On ne devrait en aucun cas manquer de prendre un petit déjeuner sur la toiture-terrasse. La vue panoramique sur la ville de lagunes est tout simplement incomparable.

Las familias reales, artistas de cine y la jetset internacional vienen una y otra vez al refugio situado directamente en el Canale Grande. El hotel es un complejo formado por un palacio antiguo y un edificio nuevo que resulta difícil de captar desde el exterior. Los clientes habituales son de la opinión que el Grandhotel, creado en 1880, es el primer destino para dormir y comer opíparamente en Venecia. Tal vez sea también el carácter despilfarrador del mobiliario – una acertada mezcla de estilos, entre rococó y arte deco – que entusiasma a los clientes y paseantes. Quien tenga la suerte de pernoctar aquí podrá experimentar desde las terrazas el "saber vivir" de Venecia: Góndolas, el silencio entre las casas, personas elegantes y mucha historia. No se debería renunciar a un desayuno en la terraza. Resulta incomparable el panorama sobre la ciudad de los canales.

Between opulence and simplicity. This interior demonstrates a successful balance of the two.

Zwischen Prunk und Schlichtheit. Das Interieur zeigt eine gelungene Gratwanderung.

Entre le faste et la simplicité. L'intérieur montre un difficile exercice d'équilibre bien réussi.

Entre la pompa y la sencillez. El interior muestra un acertado de la cresta.

Function room behind the lobby and bar.

Veranstaltungsraum hinter der Lobby und Bar.

Salle de manifestations derrière le lobby et bar.

Sala de la reuniones detrás del vestíbulo y del bar.

As if time stood still: suites and rooms in the hotel. There are approximately 200 rooms of accommodation.

Als wäre die Zeit stehen geblieben: Suiten und Zimmer im Hotel. Insgesamt gibt es rund 200 Räume zum Wohnen.

Comme si le temps s'était arrêté : les suites et les chambres de l'hôtel. Ce dernier offre en tout environ 200 pièces d'habitation.

Como si se hubiera detenido el tiempo: Suites y habitaciones del hotel. Existen aproximademente 200 habitaciones disponibles.

A room with a view: view from one of the suites. Opulent craftsmanship from floor to walls to ceiling.

Zimmer mit Aussicht. Blick aus einer der Suiten. Prunkvolle Handwerkskunst vom Boden über die Wände bis zur Decke.

Chambres avec vue. Vue depuis l'une des suites. Un artisanat festueux du sol jusqu'au plafond, sans oublier les murs.

Habitaciones con vistas. Perspectiva desde una de las suites. Fastuosa artesanía desde el suelo hasta el techo pasando por las paredes.

Danieli

Venice, Italy

A house for the rich and beautiful that could have come out of a storybook: This renovated 14th century palazzo attracts guests with the highest level of modern hotel comfort and an interior reminiscent of earlier times. One can cross the opulent atrium to the gilded staircase to reach the 221 rooms and 12 suites in two divided buildings. Whether one observes the pink marble, the painted glasswork, the chandeliers made of Murano glass or the gilded columns—this luxury hotel is synonymous with elegance and romance. Originally built for the Italian noble family Dandolo, the palace, in Gothic style, housed princes, cardinals and ambassadors from a number of countries. In 1822, Giuseppe Del Niel rented a part of the noble house and made it into a hotel with the nickname Danieli. Today, celebrities and more minor luminaries still enjoy staying here, only a few steps from the Piazza San Marco, with a view of the Canale Grande.

Ein Haus für die Reichen und Schönen wie es im Buche steht: Dieser restaurierter Palazzo aus dem 14. Jahrhundert lockt die Gäste mit modernstem Hotelkomfort und einem Interieur aus früheren Zeiten. Von dem pompösen Atrium gelangt man über eine vergoldete Treppe in die 221 Zimmer und 12 Suiten in zwei Gebäuden. Ob rosa Marmor, Glasmalereien, Kronleuchter aus Murano-Glas oder vergoldete Säulen – die Luxusherberge ist ein Synonym für Eleganz und Romantik. Einst für die berühmte italienische Adelsfamilie Dandolo erbaut, beherbergte der Palast im Gotik-Stil Prinzen, Kardinäle und Botschafter aus aller Herren Ländern. 1822 mietete Giuseppe Del Niel einen Teil des noblen Hauses und machte es zu einem Hotel mit seinem Spitznamen Danieli. So lassen es sich auch heute noch die Stars und Sternchen nicht nehmen, nur wenige Schritte vom Markusplatz mit Blick auf den Canale Grande zu nächtigen.

Un parfait exemple de résidence pour les riches et les beautés de ce monde : ce palais restauré du XIVe siècle attire ses hôtes avec le confort le plus moderne que puisse offrir un hôtel et un intérieur très ancien. L'atrium pompeux mène, via un escalier doré, aux 221 chambres et 12 suites réparties sur deux bâtiments. Que ce soit avec le marbre rose, les peintures sur verre, les lustres en verre de Murano ou les colonnes dorées, cette auberge de luxe est synonyme d'élégance et de romantisme. Jadis bâti pour la célèbre famille noble italienne Dandolo, le palais d'architecture gothique hébergea des princes, cardinaux et ambassadeurs des quatre coins du monde. En 1822, Giuseppe Del Niel décida de louer une partie de cette résidence noble et la transforma en hôtel qu'il baptisa « Danieli », son surnom. Aujourd'hui encore, les stars et les starlettes ne se privent pas du plaisir d'y passer la nuit, à quelques pas de la place Saint-Marc, et avec une vue imprenable sur le Canale Grande.

Un lugar para ricos y hermosos, tal y como marcan los cánones: Este palacio restaurado del siglo 14 atrae a los clientes con el más moderno confort hotelero y un interior de otra época. Desde el ostentoso atrio se accede a las 221 habitaciones y 12 suites, distribuidas en dos edificios, a través de unas escaleras doradas. Bien sea el mármol rosa, las pinturas sobre cristal, las lámparas de corona de cristal de Murano o las columnas doradas, el hospedaje de lujo es sinónimo de elegancia y romanticismo. Construido antiguamente para la famosa familia aristocrática italiana Dandolo, el palacio de estilo gótico alojó a príncipes, cardenales y embajadores de todo los países. Giuseppe Del Niel alquiló una parte de la noble casa en 1822 y la convirtió en un hotel con el nombre de su apodo, Danieli. Así, las estrellas y aspirantes a ello no dejan de privarse aún hoy de pernoctar a pocos pasos de la plaza de San Marcos con vista del Gran Canal.

The view of St. Mark's Square can be enjoyed from the roof restaurant "Terrazza Danieli", among other vantage points in the hotel.

Den Blick auf den Markusplatz gewährt nicht nur das Dachrestaurant „Terrazza Danieli".

Le restaurant en terrasse « Terrazza Danieli » n'est pas le seul à garantir la vue sur la place Saint-Marc.

El restaurante de la azotea "Terrazza Danieli" no sólo permite una vista de la plaza de San Marcos.

Whether chandeliers, frescoes, or gilded columns—a breeze of past eras by drifts through this noble palace.

Ob Kronleuchter, Freskenmalereien oder vergoldete Säulen – in diesem Nobelpalast weht ein Lüftchen vergangener Epochen.

Les lustres, fresques ou colonnes dorées confèrent à ce palais noble un soupçon de l'atmosphère des époques passées.

Bien sean lámparas de corona, pinturas de frescos o columnas doradas, en este noble palacio sopla un airecillo de otras épocas.

San Clemente Palace
Venice, Italy

Merely ten sailing minutes away from Venice, the Renaissance building raises itself in the centre of the private island San Clemente. The settlement of the small island began as early as 1131 although the former cloister and later mental hospital originated in the 17th century. During the renovation period, the architects showed their deep respect for the historically-rich past and natural treasures of the island. The elegant entrance hall is furnished with velvet and damask. 116 rooms and 89 suites are situated on the floors of the five-star hotel. All rooms are equipped with two telephones and a high-speed Internet facility. The complex also contains a Beauty-Centre, a three-hole golfing grounds and tennis courts. Lovers of good food enjoy the four restaurants of the house: In the "Ca' dei Frati" there is an à-la-Carte menu with a view onto the Piazza San Marco or in the "La Laguna" there is a buffet directly at the swimming pool. Unique to the hotel is the building's "own" church, which can also be used for wedding services and baptisms.

Nur zehn Bootsminuten von Venedig entfernt, erhebt sich der Renaissance-Bau mitten auf der Privatinsel San Clemente. Schon 1131 begann die Besiedlung des kleinen Eilands, wobei das Gebäude des ehemaligen Klosters und späteren Nervenheilanstalt aus dem 17. Jahrhundert stammt. Bei der Renovierung bewiesen die Architekten großen Respekt vor der historischen Vergangenheit und den Naturschätzen der Insel. Die elegante Eingangshalle ist mit Samt und Damast ausgestattet, auf den Etagen des Fünf-Sterne-Hotels verteilen sich 116 Zimmer und 89 Suiten, jeweils mit zwei Telefonen und einem High-Speed-Internet-Anschluss. Zur Anlage gehören ebenfalls ein Beauty-Center, ein Drei-Loch-Golfplatz und Tennisplätze. Gaumenfreude genießen heißt es in den vier Restaurants des Hauses: So gibt es im „Ca' dei Frati" à-la-Carte-Menüs mit Blick auf die Piazza San Marco oder im „La Laguna" ein Buffet direkt am Swimmingpool. Einzigartig ist die „hoteleigene" Kirche, die auch für Trauungen und Taufen zur Verfügung steht.

A dix minutes de bateau seulement de Venise se dresse la construction style Renaissance en plein centre de l'île privée de San Clemente. En 1131 déjà commença le peuplement de cet îlot ; l'origine du bâtiment de l'ancien monastère, qui fut plus tard transformé en hôpital psychiatrique, remonte au 17e siècle. Tout au long de la rénovation, les architectes ont fait montre d'un grand respect de l'histoire et des trésors naturels de l'île. L'élégant hall d'entrée est pourvu de velours et de damas. Aux étages de cet hôtel cinq étoiles, on retrouve 116 chambres et 89 suites équipées chacune de deux téléphones et d'un accès Internet grande vitesse. Le complexe comprend également un centre de beauté, un terrain de golf à trois trous et des courts de tennis. Les gourmets se régaleront dans les quatre restaurants de l'établissement : par exemple, menu à la carte au « Ca' dei Frati », qui offre une belle vue sur la Piazza San Marco, ou buffet au bord de la piscine à « La Laguna ». Une des particularités de l'hôtel est « son » église que l'on peut réserver pour les mariages religieux et les baptêmes.

Situado a sólo diez minutos en barco de Venecia, el edificio del renacimiento se erige en el centro de la isla privada San Clemente. El pequeño islote comenzó ya a poblarse en tan temprana fecha del año 1131, aunque el edificio del antiguo convento y posterior clínica psiquiátrica proviene del siglo 17. Los arquitectos mostraron en la restauración un gran respeto por el pasado histórico y tesoros naturales de la isla. El elegante hall de entrada se halla provisto de terciopelo y damasco, y por las plantas del hotel de cinco estrellas se distribuyen 116 habitaciones y 89 suites, cada una de las cuales cuenta con dos teléfonos y una conexión de alta velocidad a Internet. La recinto posee también un centro de belleza, un campo de golf con tres hoyos y pistas de tenis. En los cuatro restaurantes de la casa puede disfrutarse de los placeres del paladar: Así, el "Ca' dei Frati" ofrece un menú a la carta con vista a la Plaza de San Marcos, o en "La Laguna" existe un buffet al borde de la piscina. La iglesia "propia del hotel" constituye una característica singular, la cual también se halla disponible para bodas y bautizos.

Venice right in view—only ten minutes by boat to the luxury hotel.

Venedig fest im Blick, geht's mit einem Boot zehn Minuten lang übers Wasser zum Luxushotel.

Venise bien à l'œil, on se rend en tout juste dix minutes de bateau à l'hôtel de luxe.

Venecia fija a la vista; en un paseo por el agua de diez minutos en barco se llega al hotel de lujo.

Pillar colonnades decorate the hall to the swimming pool and directly to the buffet in the restaurants "La Laguna"—completely in Renaissance style.

Säulenkolonnaden schmücken den Gang zum Swimmingpool und direkt zum Buffet des Restaurants „La Laguna" – ganz im Renaissance-Stil.

Des colonnades parent l'allée vers la piscine et mènent directement au buffet du restaurant « La Laguna » – style Renaissance parfaitement reproduit !

Las galerías de columnas adornan el pasillo que va a la piscina y directamente al buffet del restaurante "La Laguna"; estilo renacentista en su totalidad.

San Clemente Palace *Venice, Italy* 153

Marble, velvet and damask—the designers did not save on anything when creating the impression of romantic and elegance.

Marmor, Samt und Damast – die Designer haben an nichts gespart, um den Eindruck von Romantik und Eleganz entstehen zu lassen.

Marbre, velours et damas – les stylistes n'ont lésiné sur rien pour que l'hôte garde l'impression de romantisme et d'élégance.

Mármol, terciopelo y damasco; los diseñadores no han escatimado en gastos para dejar una impresión de romanticismo y elegancia.

Choupana Hills Resort & Spa

Madeira, Portugal

Nestled in the subtropical forests of Madeira between mimosa and eucalyptus trees, 500 metres above sea level with a fantastic view of the Atlantic Ocean, lies this luxury resort. Guests might be left wondering whether or not they're in Asia rather than on this peaceful, flowery island in the expanse of the Atlantic. Indeed, French architects Michel de Camaret and Didier Lefort were inspired by the Aman resorts of Asia in their design of the hotel complex. They've created 34 villas comprising 60 deluxe rooms and 4 generous suites. Their concept includes an airy reception area flooded with natural light, and a spacious pool area decorated with exotic plants. It's a concept which promises every guest stillness, seclusion and perfect relaxation in hotel's own spa.

Eingebettet in die subtropischen Wälder Madeiras zwischen Mimosen und Eukalyptusbäumen, 500 Meter hoch mit einem hinreißenden Blick auf den Atlantischen Ozean, liegt dieses Luxusresort, das seine Gäste glauben macht, sie befänden sich in Asien und nicht mitten in der Weite des Atlantik auf der viel gerühmten Blumeninsel. Für die Konzeption des offenen licht- und luftdurchfluteten Empfangsbereichs, der von exotischen Grünpflanzen gesäumten, weitläufigen Poolanlage und der 34 Villen, die 60 Deluxezimmer und 4 großzügige Suiten beherbergen, ließen sich die französischen Architekten Michel de Camaret und Didier Lefort von den asiatischen Amanresorts inspirieren. Ein Konzept, das sich auch in der Philosophie widerspiegelt, die dem Gast Stille, Abgeschiedenheit und perfekte Verwöhnprogramme im hauseigenen Spa verheißt.

Niché dans les forêts subtropicales de Madère, entre les mimosas et les eucalyptus, cet hôtel de luxe situé sur une hauteur de 500 mètres, donne l'impression aux visiteurs qu'ils passent un séjour en Asie alors qu'ils se trouvent au beau milieu de l'Atlantique sur cette île renommée pour sa végétation florale. Pour concevoir l'espace d'accueil ouvert, éclairé et aéré, la piscine spacieuse bordée de plantes vertes exotiques, ainsi que 34 villas comprenant 60 chambres de luxe et 4 grandes suites, les architectes français Michel de Camaret et Didier Lefort se sont inspirés des Amanresorts asiatiques. Ce concept se retrouve aussi dans la philosophie locale, qui promet aux visiteurs du calme dans un lieu retiré avec un programme parfait pour les choyer dans le spa de l'hôtel.

Incrustado entre mimosas y eucaliptos de las selvas subtropicales de Madeira, a una altura de 500 metros y con una vista fascinante de la bahía de Funchal se encuentra este complejo de lujo que invita a creer a sus clientes que podrían hallarse en Asia y no en el centro del vasto océano Atlántico, en la cacareada isla de las flores. Los arquitectos franceses Michel de Camaret y Didier Lefort se inspiraron en los complejos asiáticos Aman para el diseño del área de recepción, abierta e inundada de luz y aire, de la amplia piscina, rodeada de plantas exóticas verdes, y de los 34 mansiones, que incluyen 60 habitaciones de lujo y 4 suites. Un diseño que también se refleja en la filosofía, y que promete al cliente silencio, aislamiento y perfectos programas de cuidado en el balneario propio del complejo hotelero.

The Asia-inspired main building houses the lounge, restaurant and spa.

Das asiatisch inspirierte Hauptgebäude beherbergt Lounge, Restaurant und Spa.

Le bâtiment principal inspiré de la culture asiatique comprend une salle de séjour, un restaurant et un spa.

El edificio principal de inspiración asiática aloja el lounge, el restaurante y el balneario.

Shimmering green mosaic stones give the pool an exotic charm. As does the use of soothing, restrained colors in the lobby.

Grünlich schimmernde Mosaiksteinchen geben dem Pool eine exotische Anmutung. Beruhigende, zurück-haltende Farben in der Lobby spiegeln die Philosophie wieder.

Les petites pierres de mosaïque d'un vert scintillant donnent à la piscine un style exotique. Les teintes apaisantes et pastelles de l'entrée reflètent la philosophie locale.

Piedrecitas de mosaico verdosas y resplandecientes confieren una estimulación exótica a la piscina. Los colores relajantes y moderados del vestíbulo reflejan la filosofía del complejo hotelero.

Total relaxation in front of the blazing open fire.

Perfekte Entspannung am lodernden Kaminfeuer.

Détente parfaite au coin du feu.

Relajación perfecta en el llameante fuego de la chimenea.

Soft colors and clear lines, in the bathrooms as well. An overwhelming view of Funchal.

Sanfte Farben, klare Linienführung auch in den Bädern. Überwältigender Blick auf die Bucht von Funchal.

Des couleurs douces, des lignes claires, jusque dans les salles de bains. Une vue spectaculaire sur la baie de Funchal.

Suaves colores, claro trazado de líneas incluso en los baños. Vista fascinante de la bahía de Funchal.

Choupana Hills Resort & Spa *Madeira, Portugal*   163

Palácio Belmonte
Lisbon, Portugal

"Hotel" is only a partially accurate description for this unique city palace. It is more of a privately-run luxury domicile with just eight very different suites, the highest possible level of intimacy and a magnificent setting. It not only served as the location of Wim Wenders's film "Lisbon Story". Marcello Mastroianni also immortalised the establishment in "Afirma Pereira". Its owner is former investment banker Frédéric Coustols, who followed his heart to the city on the Tejo. During his search for a new place to live, he initially bought the property sight unseen, before realising: it was too large and too much of a shame to use only as his private house. Thus, his idea of turning it into a hotel was born, as was his passion for carefully renovating the historical building. The result is an accommodation for discerning individualists who enjoy the very personal atmosphere perhaps even more than the round-the-clock service.

„Hotel" ist für das einzigartige Stadtpalais nur bedingt zutreffend. Viel eher ist es ein privat geführtes Luxusdomizil mit nur acht ganz unterschiedlichen Suiten, höchster Intimität und grandioser Kulisse. Es diente nicht nur Wim Wenders als Drehort zu seiner „Lisbon Story", auch Marcello Mastroianni setzte dem Anwesen in „Afirma Pereira" ein Denkmal. Eigentümer ist der ehemalige Investmentbanker Frédéric Coustols, den die Liebe an die Stadt am Tejo führte. Bei der Suche nach einer neuen Bleibe kaufte er das Anwesen zunächst unbesehen, um später festzustellen: zu groß und auch zu schade, um es nur für sich privat zu nutzen. So entstand die Idee zum Hotel und gleichzeitig die Leidenschaft, das geschichtsträchtige Gebäude behutsam zu renovieren. Herausgekommen ist eine Adresse für anspruchsvolle Individualisten, die weniger auf den 24-Stundenservice als auf sehr persönliche Atmosphäre aus sind.

Le mot « Hôtel » est un qualificatif convenable seulement en partie pour ce palais citadin hors du commun ; c'est plutôt une résidence de luxe en mains privées comportant huit suites seulement dont chacune est totalement différente de l'autre, et offrant à ses hôtes une très grande intimité et des coulisses grandioses. Wim Wenders l'a choisie à bon escient comme cadre pour tourner son film « Lisbon Story ». De même, Marcello Mastroianni l'a rendue inoubliable dans le film « Afirma Pereira ». Son propriétaire est l'ancien banquier d'affaires Frédéric Coustols que l'amour conduisit à Lisbonne. A la recherche d'une nouvelle demeure, il acheta d'abord la propriété sans l'avoir auparavant visitée pour constater plus tard qu'elle était trop grande et que ce serait aussi un peu dommage de l'utiliser à des fins strictement privées. C'est ainsi qu'est née l'idée d'en faire un hôtel, et en même temps la passion de rénover ce bâtiment historique avec ménagement. Il en résulta une adresse qui, aujourd'hui, est le point de rencontre des individualistes exigeants qui accordent moins d'importance au service 24h/24 qu'à l'atmosphère très personnalisée.

Al singular palacio de ciudad sólo puede asignársele el término "hotel" con restricciones. Más bien se trata de un hospedaje de lujo gestionado de forma privada, con sólo ocho suites, pero completamente distintas, máxima intimidad y un aspecto grandioso. El mismo no sólo sirvió a Wim Wenders como lugar de rodaje de su "Lisbon Story", sino que también dejó su impronta en la mansión Marcello Mastroianni con "Afirma Pereira". Su propietario es el antiguo banquero de inversiones Frédéric Coustols, a quien su amor por la ciudad lo condujo al Tejo. En la búsqueda de un nuevo hogar compró la mansión sin reparar demasiado en ella al principio, para darse cuenta después que era demasiado grande y que también era una pena utilizarla sólo para su uso privado. Así surgió la idea del hotel y al mismo tiempo la intención de renovar cuidadosamente un edificio preñado de historia. El resultado ha sido un lugar para exigentes individualistas que valoran más una atmósfera muy personal que un servicio las 24 horas.

Guests here enter a different world, far from the usual hotel experience. The atmosphere is more like a visit with friends in a majestic city palace.

Als Gast taucht man hier in eine andere Welt, fernab der üblichen Hotellerie. Die Atmosphäre ist eher wie bei Freunden in einem majestätischen Stadtpalais.

L'hôte immerge ici dans un autre monde, loin de l'hôtellerie conventionnelle. Il y règne une atmosphère plutôt comme entre amis, dans un palais citadin majestueux.

Los clientes se sumergen aquí en un mundo distinto de la parafernalia hotelera habitual. La atmósfera es más bien de amigos en un majestuoso palacio de ciudad.

From the first moment in one of the eight expressively-decorated suites or on one of the terraces, guests leave their occupational stress and hectic city life behind.

Spätestens, wenn man in einer der acht gefühlvoll eingerichteten Suiten oder auf einer der Terrassen angekommen ist, lässt man jeden beruflichen Stress und Großstadthektik hinter sich.

Au plus tard en entrant dans l'une des huit suites, qui ont été aménagées avec beaucoup de doigté, ou en prenant place sur l'une des terrasses, vous oublierez à jamais le stress professionnel et l'agitation des grandes villes.

El estrés del trabajo y el bullicio de la gran ciudad desaparecen, como muy tarde, cuando se accede a una de las ocho suites amuebladas con gran sensibilidad o a alguna de las terrazas.

Palácio Belmonte *Lisbon, Portugal* 167

Gran Hotel La Florida

Barcelona, Spain

After four years of renovation, Barcelona reclaimed its formerly most historical hotel in the summer of 2003. Perched atop Tibidabo, overlooking the city and the Mediterranean Sea, the hotel with a long tradition shines anew. With only 74 rooms and suites, it is a deluxe retreat with a private atmosphere, ideal for stress-free conventions or a private weekend with a shopping spree in the city and wellness treatments in the fresh mountain air. The new owners, the Stein Group, endeavoured to preserve as much of its original charm as possible, while at the same time offering innovation with regard to architecture, design and recreational activity. As a result, there are eight design suites that have been decorated by international designers and artists, among them Cristina Macaya, Hans Duettmann, Rebecca Horn and Yannick Vu. The wellness centre is extravagantly luxurious for an establishment of this size, with its 37-metre long pool leading outdoors from within a glass, steel and wooden addition, and offering swimmers a permanent panorama of the city and the sea.

Nach vierjähriger Renovierung hat Barcelona seit dem Sommer 2003 eines seiner ehemals traditionsreichsten Hotels zurückerhalten. Auf dem Tibidabo, erhaben über der Stadt und dem Mittelmeer strahlt das einstige Traditionshaus nun in neuem Glanz. Mit nur 74 Zimmern und Suiten bleibt es ein Luxusrefugium mit privater Atmosphäre, ideal für die stressfreie Tagung oder fürs private Wochenende mit Einkaufsbummel in der Stadt und Wohlfühlprogramm in luftigen Höhen. Den neuen Eigentümern, Stein-Group, lag daran, soviel wie möglich des ursprünglichen Charmes zu erhalten, gleichzeitig jedoch in Architektur, Design und Freizeitangebot Innovatives zu bieten. So gibt es acht Designsuiten, die internationale Gestalter und Künstler eingerichtet haben, unter ihnen Cristina Macaya, Hans Duettmann, Rebecca Horn oder Yannick Vu. Für ein Haus dieser Größe geradezu verschwenderisch luxuriös ist das Wellnesszentrum mit seinem 37 Meter langen Pool, der aus einem modernen Glas-Stahl-Holz-Anbau ins Freie führt und den Schwimmenden stets eine Panoramaaussicht über die Stadt und aufs Meer bietet.

Après quatre ans de travaux de construction, Barcelone a retrouvé depuis l'été 2003 l'un de ses hôtels les plus riches en tradition. En bordure du Tibidabo, dominant la ville et la mer Méditerranée, la demeure traditionnelle d'antant resplendit de mille feux. Avec seulement 74 chambres et suites de style, cet hôtel reste un refuge de luxe à atmosphère privée, idéal pour des séjours loin du stress ou pour des week-ends privés avec shopping en ville et programme de wellness dans les hauteurs éthérées. Les nouveaux propriétaires appartenant au Stein-Group ont tout mis en œuvre pour préserver autant que possible le charme initial, essayant toutefois aussi d'offrir quelque chose d'innovateur en matière d'architecture, de design et de loisirs. Ainsi, on y trouvera huit suites aménagées par des designers et des artistes internationaux, dont notamment Cristina Macaya, Hans Duettmann, Rebecca Horn ou Yannick Vu. Pour un établissement de cette taille, le centre de wellness est presque démesurément luxurieux avec sa piscine d'une longueur de 37 mètres. Sa construction moderne en verre-acier-bois conduit les visiteurs à l'air libre et offre en permanence aux nageurs une vue panoramique sur la ville et sur la mer.

Tras cuatro años de restauración, Barcelona ha recuperado desde el verano de 2003 uno de sus hoteles más tradicionales en el pasado. Situado sobre el Tibidabo, elevado por encima de la ciudad y el Mediterráneo, la antigua casa tradicional irradia ahora un nuevo esplendor. Con sólo 74 habitaciones y suites continúa siendo un refugio de lujo con atmósfera privada, ideal para conferencias sin estrés o para un fin de semana privado y realizar una visita a la ciudad para ir de compras y un programa relajante en las aireadas alturas. Los nuevos propietarios, el Grupo Stein, consideraron importante conservar el máximo encanto original posible, pero ofrecer al mismo tiempo aspectos innovadores en su arquitectura, diseño y actividades de ocio. Así pues, existen ocho suites de diseño, concebidas por diseñadores y artistas internacionales, entre los que se cuentan Cristina Macaya, Hans Duettmann, Rebecca Horn o Yannick Vu. El centro de relajación es francamente un lujoso derroche para una casa de este tamaño, con su piscina de 37 metros que conduce al exterior a través de un moderno edificio contiguo de cristal, acero y madera, y que siempre ofrece a los nadadores una vista panorámica de la ciudad y del mar.

Behind the new building containing the pool, wellness centre and bar, the totally renovated hotel building rises in new lustre. From the tower suites, one can see the Pyrenees Mountains on a clear day.

Hinter dem Neubau mit Pool, Wellnesszentrum und Bar erhebt sich das rundum erneuerte Hotelgebäude. Von den Turmsuiten aus sieht man bei klarem Wetter bis zu den Pyrenäen.

Derrière la nouvelle construction avec piscine, centre de wellness et bar se dresse le complexe hôtelier entièrement rénové. Depuis les suites tourelles, on a par temps clair une belle vue sur les Pyrénées.

Detrás del nuevo edificio con piscina, centro de relajación y bar se erige el edificio del hotel, restaurado en su totalidad. Desde las suites con torreones pueden observarse los Pirineos si las condiciones meteorológicas lo permiten.

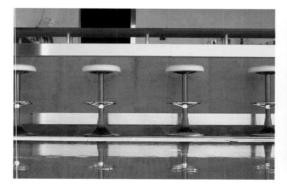

View of the edgeless swimming pool and of one of the designer suites with two bedrooms, and private terrace, complete with outdoor Jacuzzi.

Blick auf das randlose Schwimmbad und in eine der Designsuiten mit zwei Schlafzimmern, privater Terrasse inklusive Freiluft-Jacuzzi.

Vue sur la piscine sans bord et dans l'une des suites design avec deux chambres à coucher et terrasse privée, y compris jacuzzi en plein air.

Vista de la piscina sin bordes y de una de las suites de diseño con dos dormitorios y terraza privada incluido jacuzzi al aire libre.

Gran Hotel La Florida *Barcelona, Spain* 171

Even the double rooms are extremely spacious. Right photos: lobby and seating arrangement in one of the hallways.

Selbst die Doppelzimmer sind ausgesprochen geräumig. Rechte Bilder: Lobby und Sitzgruppe in einem der Flure.

Même les chambres doubles sont très spacieuses. Images de droite : lobby et coin-salon dans l'un des couloirs.

Incluso las habitaciones dobles son realmente espaciosas. Imágenes de la derecha: Vestíbulo y grupo de asientos en uno de los pasillos.

Hesperia
Madrid, Spain

Pastel colors, warm, clear, simple, and thus shifting the focus to individual details—this inimitable style of Pascua Ortega alone, one of the most popular Spanish designers, elevates the "Hesperia" above the ranks of conventional deluxe hotels. Grid-like rectangles, climbing upward, alternate with lines and lights that place individual pictures, floral arrangements or design icons in the centre of meditative observation. In this private world of open, luxurious lobbies, 137 rooms and 34 suites having more of a classical tone, are distributed over nine floors. Just as remarkable: the innovative eloquence of the service personnel, who, during the hiring process, even have acting lessons. In the kitchen, as well, the hotel makes an impact, with its much decorated Catalonian master chef Santi Santamaria. All in all, luxury worth celebrating—and not only for the eye.

Pastellfarben warm, klar und übersichtlich und somit konzentriert auf einzelne Details den Fokus lenkend – schon dieser unverkennbare Stil von Pascua Ortega, einem der führenden spanischen Designer, hebt das „Hesperia" aus der Riege gängiger Deluxe-Hotels heraus. Gitterartige Rechtecke, die nach oben streben, wechseln sich ab mit Linienführungen und Lichtinstallationen, die einzelne Bilder, Blumengestecke oder Design-Ikonen in den Mittelpunkt meditativer Betrachtung rücken. In diese eigene Welt offener luxuriöser Hallen fügen sich über neun Stockwerke hinweg 137 Zimmer und 34 Suiten, die mehr eine klassische Note besitzen. Kaum weniger bemerkenswert: die innovative Eloquenz des Servicepersonals, das sich bei der Auswahl sogar schauspielerischer Übungen unterzog. Auch kulinarisch setzt das Haus höchstdekorierte Akzente mit dem katalanischen Meisterkoch Santi Santamaria. Alles in allem ein zelebrierter Luxus – nicht nur für das Auge.

Couleurs pastel, chaleureux, clair et dégagé, et ainsi concentré sur des détails précis, guidant le regard sur ces derniers – Ce style incomparable de Pascua Ortega, l'un des stylistes espagnols les plus renommés, singularise le « Hesperia » parmi les hôtels grand luxe courants. Des rectangles en forme de grilles montrant vers le haut alternent avec des lignes et installations lumineuses qui mettent des tableaux, compositions florales ou icônes de style individuels au centre de l'analyse méditative. Ce monde pour soi de foyers luxurieux ouverts abrite, sur neuf étages, 137 chambres et 34 suites qui ont une note plutôt classique. Egalement remarquable au même titre est l'éloquence innovatrice du personnel de service qui a même dû faire montre de ses talents de comédien dans le cadre de la procédure de sélection. L'établissement impose également de nouveaux standards sur le plan culinaire avec les créations, qui ont obtenu les plus grandes distinctions, du maître-cuisinier catalan Santi Santamaria. En tout et pour tout, la célébration du luxe – pas seulement pour les yeux.

Cálido, diáfano y claro como el color pastel, y por tanto orientando el foco de atención de forma concentrada a los diferentes detalles; este estilo inconfundible de Pascual Ortega, uno de los diseñadores españoles más destacados, permite que el "Hesperia" sobresalga de los hoteles de lujo concencionales. Rectángulos con forma de reja que se extienden hacia arriba alternan con trazados de líneas y sistemas de luces que sitúan a cuadros individuales, centros florales o iconos de diseño en el punto central de la meditación contemplativa. En este mundo autónomo de lujosas galerías abiertas se distribuyen a lo largo de nueve plantas 137 habitaciones y 34 suites más bien de carácter clásico. Apenas le va a la zaga la elocuencia refinada del personal de servicio, al cual se le impartio incluso clases de interpretación tras el proceso de selección. La casa también destaca en el aspecto culinario por motivos altamente decorativos creados por el jefe de cocina Santi Santamaria. Resumiendo, un lujo para ser disfrutado no sólo con la vista.

Moorish flair with a light well in the lobby. Clear shapes and lines with aesthetic allure create the prevailing ambience.

Maurisch anmutend ein Lichthof in der Lobby. Immer wieder dominieren klare ästhetische Formen und Linien.

Une cour vitrée donnant une impression mauresque dans le lobby. On rencontre toujours et partout des formes et lignes claires et dominantes d'une beauté captivante.

En el vestíbulo existe un patio de luces con encanto moruno. Las formas y líneas claras dominan el ambiente confiriendo un carácter estético.

Openness and transparency characterize the style of the hotel. Even a view into the mostly hidden kitchen artistry in the gourmet restaurant is allowed.

Offenheit und Transparenz kennzeichnen den Stil des Hauses. Selbst der Blick auf die zumeist verborgenen Künste des Gourmetrestaurants wird nicht verwehrt.

Ouverture et transparence caractérisent le style de l'établissement. On n'y interdit même pas un bref coup d'œil sur les arts le plus souvent cachés du restaurant gastronomique.

La casa se caracteriza por un estilo abierto y transparente. Incluso tampoco se impide observar las obras de arte del restaurante gourmet no expuestas generalmente.

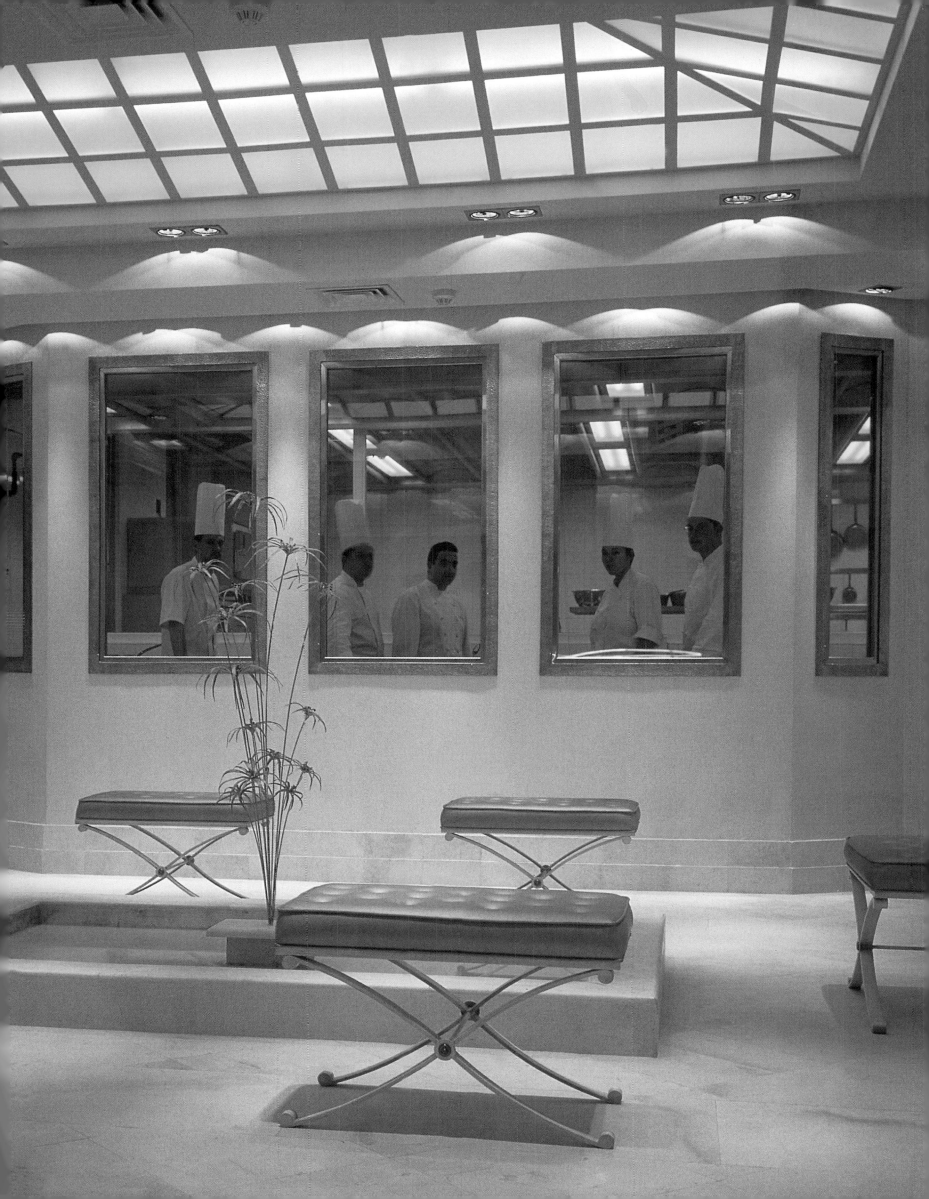

Ornaments are rare. But where they do appear, they are the focus of attention. Even in places where people meet, an exquisite style characterizes the ambience.

Ornamente sind rar. Doch wenn, dann richtet sich die ganze Konzentration darauf. Auch dort, wo man sich trifft, bestimmt ein erlesener Stil das Ambiente.

Les ornements sont rares. Cependant, quand il en existe, ils captivent tous les regards. En outre, un style raffiné caractérise l'atmosphère des endroits de rencontre.

No abundan los adornos, pero aquellos existentes se adueñan de la concentración por completo. El ambiente se halla impregnado de un estilo selecto en cualquier rincón.

Rio Real Golf Hotel
Marbella, Spain

On the Mediterranean Sea, nestled in the mountains of Sierra Bermeja, just five minutes from the bustle of Marbella, lies this relaxation retreat. As early as 1965, Javier Arana constructed the 18-hole golf course with a view of the sea, which, ever since, has been attracting more than just sports fans to Andalusia. Interior designer Pascua Ortega has combined modern with classic elements in Marbella's first boutique hotel. The 30 rooms and suites of the five-star deluxe establishment are furnished in varying styles, and offer a view of the mountains, palm trees and ocean. In the "Río Real Restaurant", chef de cuisine Paco Naranjo and his team serve Mediterranean delicacies as well as international cuisine in an exclusive atmosphere, characterized by dark wood and cool steel.

Am Mittelmeer, zwischen den Bergen von Sierra Bermeja, nur fünf Minuten vom geschäftigen Treiben Marbellas entfernt, liegt diese Oase der Entspannung. Schon 1965 legte Javier Arana den 18-Loch-Golfplatz mit Blick aufs Wasser an, der seitdem nicht nur Sportbegeisterte nach Andalusien lockt. Interior-Designer Pascua Ortega kombinierte in diesem ersten Boutiquehotel Marbellas Moderne mit Klassik. Die 30 Zimmer und Suiten des Fünf-Sterne-Deluxe-Hotels sind verschieden eingerichtet und bieten einen Blick auf Berge, Palmen und Meer. Im „Río Real Restaurant" serviert das Team um den Chef de Cuisine, Paco Naranjo, Köstlichkeiten der mediterranen und internationalen Küche im exklusiven Ambiente inmitten von dunklem Holz und kühlem Stahl.

Cette oasis de détente est située sur la mer Méditerranée, entre les montagnes de la Sierra Bermeja, à cinq minutes du centre des affaires de Marbella. Conçu par l'architecte Javier Arena et ouvert en 1965, ce terrain de golf de 18 trous avec vue imprenable sur la mer n'attire pas seulement les passionnés du green en Andalousie. L'architecte d'intérieur Pascua Ortega a combiné dans ce premier hôtel-boutique de Marbella le moderne au classique. Chacune des 30 chambres et suites de cet hôtel de luxe cinq étoiles est aménagée individuellement et offre une vue de tout premier plan sur les montagnes, les palmiers et la mer. Le chef de cuisine Paco Naranjo et son équipe servent au « Río Real Restaurant » des spécialités de la cuisine méditerranéenne et internationale dans une ambiance exclusive sur toile de fond de bois sombres et d'acier froid.

Este oasis de relajación se encuentra situado en el mediterráneo, entre las montañas de Sierra Bermeja, y sólo a cinco minutos del bullicio comercial de Marbella. Ya en 1965 inauguró Javier Arana el campo de golf de 18 hoyos con vista al mar, el cual no sólo atrae desde entonces a Andalucía a aficionados del deporte. El diseñador de interiores Pascua Ortega combinó tendencias modernas y clásicas en este primer hotel-boutique de Marbella. Las 30 habitaciones y suites del hotel de lujo de cinco estrellas se hallan equipadas de diferente forma y ofrecen una vista de las montañas, de las palmeras y del mar. En el restaurante "Río Real", el equipo que rodea al jefe de cocina, Paco Naranjo, sirve exquisiteces del mediterráneo y platos internacionales en un ambiente exclusivo rodeado de madera oscura y acero frío.

First, hit golf balls between hills, slopes and palm trees, then relax in the hotel's soft armchairs—all with a view of the Mediterranean.

Erst die weißen Bälle zwischen Hügeln, Hängen und Palmen einlochen, dann im weichen Sessel des Hotels entspannen — die Sicht aufs Mittelmeer immer im Blick.

La devise est : on tape d'abord les balles blanches entre les collines, les pentes et les palmiers, puis l'heure est à la détente dans un des fauteuils moelleux de l'hôtel — la vue sur la mer Méditerranée toujours en ligne de mire.

Primero meter las bolas blancas entre colinas, pendientes y palmeras, luego relajarse en las cómodas butacas del hotel, y la vista del mediterráneo siempre en el fondo.

Whether it is the flickering of the fireplace in the Albatros Suite or the scent of flowers in the lobby—Pascua Ortega is responsible for the design.

Ob das Funkeln des Kaminfeuers in der Albatros Suite oder der Blumenduft in der Lobby — Pascua Ortega zeichnet für das Design verantwortlich.

Qu'il s'agisse du feu de cheminée dans la suite Albatros ou de l'effluve des fleurs dans le lobby, un seul nom est responsable du design : Pascua Ortega.

Bien sea el centelleo del fuego de la chimenea en la suite Albatros o el olor a flor en el vestíbulo, Pascua Ortega deja su firma como responsable del diseño.

One of the many places guests can enjoy nature is in the inviting pool on the roof of the luxury hotel.

Natur pur genießen die Gäste nicht nur im einladenden Pool auf dem Dach der Luxusherberge.

La piscine accueillante située sur le toit de cette résidence de luxe n'est pas le seul endroit où les hôtes peuvent profiter de la nature pure.

Los clientes no sólo disfrutan de auténtica naturaleza en la insinuante piscina de la azotea del hospedaje de lujo.

Ca's Xorc

Mallorca, Spain

This small estate hotel on Mallorca was once an olive mill, situated in the mountains of Soller. German software entrepreneur Klaus Plönzke renovated the structure, breathing new life into it. His daughter Britta runs the hotel. Created in the Mallorcan style, Ca's Xorc is an oasis of tranquillity—surrounded by well-tended gardens with palm trees, olive trees and fountains. This nested country house harbours only 13 double rooms, furnished in a rustic, Mediterranean manner. In pleasant weather, people meet on the terrace and enjoy a magnificent view of the mountains and surrounding sea, or swim around the pool, which is built into the side of a hill.

Das kleine Finca-Hotel auf Mallorca war früher eine Olivenölmühle und liegt in den Bergen von Soller. Wachgeküßt und umgebaut hat sie der deutsche Software-Unternehmer Klaus Plönzke, dessen Tochter Britta das Hotel führt. In mallorquinischer Baukunst erstellt, ist Ca's Xorc eine Oase der Ruhe — umgeben von einer gepflegten Gartenanlage mit Palmen, Olivenbäumen und Brunnen. Nur 13 rustikal-mediterran ausgestaltete Doppelzimmer hat das verschachtelte Landhaus. Bei schönem Wetter trifft man sich auf der Terrasse und genießt einen Traumblick auf die Berge und das umliegende Meer. Oder man dreht ein paar Runden im Pool, der in einen Hang hineingebaut wurde.

Le petit hôtel Finca en Majorque était naguère un moulin d'huile d'olive et se situe sur les collines de Soller. C'est Klaus Plönzke, entrepreneur allemand dans le domaine des logiciels, dont la fille Britta gère l'hôtel, qui l'a réveillé et transformé. Construit en architecture majorquine, Ca's Xorc est une oasis de tranquillité entourée d'un jardin bien entretenu avec palmiers, oliviers et fontaines. Cette maison de campagne imbriquée offre seulement 13 chambres doubles aménagées selon un style méditerranéen rustique. Par beau temps, on se rencontre sur la terrasse et jouit d'une magnifique vue sur les montagnes et la mer environnante. Ou bien on fait quelques brassées dans la piscine qui a été construite sur un talus.

La pequeña finca-hotel de Mallorca era un molino de aceite de oliva en el pasado y se encuentra situada en la sierra de Soller. El empresario de software alemán Klaus Plönzke lo descubrió y restauró y ahora su hija Britta gestiona el hotel. Construido en arquitectura mallorquina, Ca's Xorc es un oasis de tranquilidad — rodeado por una cuidada zona ajardinada que contiene palmeras, olivos y pozos. La finca entrelazada sólo dispone de 13 habitaciones dobles diseñadas en estilo rústico mediterráneo. Cuando hay buen tiempo queda uno en la terraza y disfruta de una vista de ensueño a la montaña y al mar circundante, o hace uno un par de largos en la piscina, construída en el interior de una pendiente.

Individual interior decoration: Each room has its own design. The study tempts readers to linger.

Individuelle Interieur-Gestaltung: Jedes Zimmer ist anders gestaltet. Die Bibliothek lädt zum Verweilen ein.

Aménagement individuel de l'intérieur : chaque chambre est aménagée individuellement. La bibliothèque invite à y passer quelque temps.

Diseño interior individual: Cada habitación está concebida de forma diferente. La biblioteca invita a permanecer dentro.

Hotel Manager Britta Plönzke found several pieces of furniture and accessories in the workshops and studios of Mallorcan craftspeople. Some of the textiles used come from Morocco.

Hotel-Chefin Britta Plönzke hat viele Möbel und Accessoires in Werkstätten und Ateliers von mallorquinischen Handwerkern gefunden. Die Textilien im Haus kommen zum Teil aus Marokko.

La patronne de l'hôtel, Britta Plönzke, a découvert un grand nombre de meubles et accessoires dans les ateliers d'artisans majorquins. Les textiles de l'établissement sont en partie originaires du Maroc.

La jefa del hotel, Britta Plönzke, encontró muchos muebles y accesorios en talleres y estudios de artesanos mallorquines. Los tejidos de la finca proceden en parte de Marruecos.

From the garden, guests have a fantastic view of the mountains and the bay of Port Soller. The pool is built into the hillside.

Vom Garten haben die Gäste einen fantastischen Blick auf die Berge und die Bucht von Port Soller. Der Pool wurde in den Hang integriert.

Depuis le jardin, les hôtes ont une vue fantastique sur les montagnes et la baie de Port Soller. La piscine a été intégrée dans le talus.

Desde el jardín, los clientes tienen una fantástica panorámica de las montañas y de la bahía de port Soller. La piscina fue integrada en la pendiente.

Ca's Xorc *Mallorca, Spain* 191

Hotel Alfonso XIII

Seville, Spain

A spectacular palace in Neomudéjar style rises from the heart of the city, not far from the Guadalquivir River and the cathedral. King Alfonso XIII, who had the building constructed in 1928, is the source of the royal hotel's name. 127 rooms and 19 suites are distributed on the floors of the noble house, where, in addition to Moorish architecture, accents of classical baroque can also be found. Whether staying in a non-smoking room or one of the eight Smart Rooms with modem and fax connections—the hotel staff are tuned to the wishes of their guests. Regional cuisine is served in the "San Fernando Restaurant", and the "Kaede" dishes up Japanese fare. Guests favouring the fresh Spanish air will enjoy taking a seat at the "San Fernando Bar", directly at the "El Patio" fountain in the courtyard.

Ein spektakulärer Palast im Neomudéjar-Baustil erhebt sich im Herzen der Stadt, nicht weit vom Fluss Guadalquivir und der Kathedrale entfernt. König Alfonso XIII., der 1928 den Bau veranlasste, verleiht der royalen Herberge seinen Namen. 127 Zimmer und 19 Suiten verteilen sich auf den Etagen des noblen Hauses, wobei sich neben maurischen Bauelementen auch Akzente des klassischen Barocks finden. Ob Nicht-Raucher-Zimmer oder die acht Smart-Zimmer mit Modem- und Fax-Anschluss – das Hotelteam hat sich auf die Wünsche seiner Gäste eingestellt. Im „San Fernando Restaurant" wird regionale Küche serviert, im „Kaede" dagegen japanische Speisen. Und wer lieber die spanische Luft genießen will, der nimmt Platz an der „San Fernando Bar", direkt am Wasserbrunnen „El Patio" im Innenhof.

Un grandiose palais, style néomudéjar, se dresse au cœur de la ville, à proximité du fleuve Guadalquivir et de la cathédrale. Ce palace royal doit son nom au roi Alfonso XIII, qui a ordonné sa construction en 1928. 127 chambres et 19 suites se répartissent sur les différents étages de cette noble résidence. Cet hôtel se targue d'éléments architecturaux mauresques combinés aux plus purs accents du baroque classique. Qu'il s'agisse de chambres non-fumeurs ou des huit chambres Smart avec connexion par modem et téléfax, l'équipe de l'hôtel répond à tous les vœux de ses invités. La cuisine régionale est servie au restaurant « San Fernando ». Le « Kaede » est réservé quant à lui aux plats japonais. Et quiconque veut inhaler l'air espagnol prendra place au bar « San Fernando », situé près de la fontaine « El Patio » dans la cour intérieure.

En el centro de la ciudad, no lejos del río Guadalquivir y la catedral, se alza este palacio espectacular en estilo neomudéjar. El rey Alfonso XIII, quien dispuso su construcción en 1928, prestó al hospedaje real su nombre. En las plantas de la noble casa se distribuyen 127 habitaciones y 19 suites, provistas de aspectos del barroco clásico junto con elementos moriscos de construcción. Bien sean en las habitaciones de no fumadores o en las ocho elegantes habitaciones con conexión de módem y fax, el personal del hotel se ha adaptado a los deseos de sus clientes. En el restaurante "San Fernando" se sirven platos regionales, no así en "Kaede", donde puede degustarse comida japonesa. Y quien prefiera disfrutar del aire español puede sentarse en el bar "San Fernando", directamente en la fuente "El Patio" del patio interior.

The King, who gave his name to the hotel, wanted it to be the most luxurious in Europe.

Das luxuriöseste *Hotel Europas sollte es nach Wunsch des Königs werden, der dem Luxushotel seinen Namen verlieh.*

Cet hôtel *de luxe qui porte le nom du roi devait devenir selon ses voeux l'hôtel le plus luxurieux d'Europe.*

El rey *tenía el deseo de que el hotel fuera el más lujoso de Europa, prestándole al mismo su nombre*

Built in *Moorish style, round arches are a continual dominant feature of the house. Guests enjoy the Spanish air at the "El Patio" fountain.*

Im maurischen *Stil erbaut, dominieren stets Rundbögen das Erscheinungsbild des Hauses. Spanische Luft genießen die Gäste am Wasserbrunnen „El Patio".*

Des arcades *mauresques dominent l'ensemble architectural de cet établissement royal. Les hôtes respireront l'air espagnol assis près de la fontaine « El Patio ».*

Construido *en estilo morisco, el aspecto del hotel está constantemente marcado por arcos de medio punto. En la fuente "El Patio" pueden disfrutar los clientes del aire español.*

Grand Resort Lagonissi
Athens, Greece

Comfort is the top priority in the large club facility, offering every luxury, of the Grand Resort Lagonissi. Only fifteen minutes from the Athens airport, this establishment offers every kind of accommodation, from mini suites to the Grand Royal suite, measuring 380 square metres. The Royal Suite offers everything you could possibly dream of: two bedrooms, an open fireplace, a private indoor and outdoor pool, and even a place for the butler you bring along. A comfortable style in step with the design of the building: a mixture of dark woods, light walls, warm lights, plush leather armchairs and choice accessories. In addition, the Club offers an abundance of leisure time activities and diverse restaurant selections. The fact that even families can find a perfect service package here almost seems marginal in comparison.

Komfort steht an oberster Stelle in der großen, allen Luxus offerierenden Club-Anlage vom Grand Resort Lagonissi. Nur eine Viertelstunde vom Athener Flughafen entfernt, stehen hier von Mini-Suiten bis hin zur 380 Quadratmeter umfassenden Grand Royal Ausgabe verschiedenste Unterkünfte zur Verfügung. Die Royal Suite bietet dabei alles, was man sich erträumen mag: zwei Schlafräume, eine offene Feuerstelle, einen eigenen Innen- und Außenpool und auch für den mitgebrachten Butler fehlt es nicht an einer Räumlichkeit. Ein komfortabler Stil, den auch das Design des Hauses mit trägt: Ein Mix aus dunklen Hölzern, hellen Wänden, warmen Lichtern, edlen Lederfauteuils und erlesenen Accessoires. Darüber hinaus lässt es der Club nicht an ungezählten Freizeit- und unterschiedlichsten Restaurantangeboten mangeln. Dass hier selbst Familien einen perfekten Rund-um-Service vorfinden, geht so beinahe schon als Randbemerkung unter.

Le confort est de première priorité dans ce Club spacieux du Grand Resort Lagonissi, qui offre tout luxe à ses visiteurs. Situé à seulement un quart d'heure de l'aéroport d'Athènes, cet hôtel met à disposition des logements très divers allant de mini-suites à une version Grand Royal pouvant atteindre 380 mètres carrés. La suite Royal présente tout ce dont on peut rêver : deux chambres à coucher, une cheminée, une piscine individuelle intérieure et extérieure. Le logement est même prévu pour votre « Butler » personnel. Le style confortable est souligné par le design de la maison : un mélange composé de boiseries sombres, de cloisons claires, de luminaires chauds, accompagnés de fauteuils en cuir et d'accessoires de choix. En outre, le Club présente une offre abondante d'activités de loisirs et des possibilités très diverses de se restaurer. Il va de soi, que même les familles pourront y trouver un service parfaitement adapté et complet.

La comodidad ocupa un lugar estelar en el gran complejo-club Grand Resort Lagonissi provisto de todos los lujos. A sólo un cuarto de hora del aeropuerto de Atenas, aquí se hallan disponibles los más diversos alojamientos, desde mini-suites hasta la suite Grand Royal, de 380 metros cuadrados de amplitud. La suite real ofrece todo lo que una persona puede soñar: Dos dormitorios, una chimenea abierta, una piscina propia interior y exterior e incluso espacio suficiente para un mayordomo propio. Un estilo cómodo con el que también está marcado el diseño de la casa: Una mezcla de maderas oscuras, paredes claras, luces cálidas, butacas nobles de cuero y accesorios selectos. Por otra parte, el club dispone de incontables ofertas de ocio y los más diversos restaurantes. El hecho de que las familias encuentran aquí un servicio completo perfecto no se considera más que una mera anécdota.

The pool on your own private terrace is just one of the comforts offered by the suites of the resort near Athens.

Der Pool auf der eigenen Terrasse ist nur eine der Annehmlichkeiten, die die Suiten des Resorts nahe Athen bieten.

Les piscines sur les terrasses personnelles sont l'un des agréments proposés dans les suites de cet hôtel à proximité d'Athènes.

La piscina en la propia terraza es sólo una de las comodidades que ofrecen las suites del complejo cercano a Atenas.

Generously-sized rooms characterize the style of the Club. And what could be finer than sinking into dreamland with a direct view of the stars?

Großzügige Räume kennzeichnen den Stil des Clubs. Und was gibt es Schöneres, als mit dem direkten Blick in die Sterne ins Reich der Träume zu versinken?

Les vastes pièces sont une caractéristique du style du Club. Et qu'y a-t-il de plus merveilleux, que de sombrer dans le monde des rêves avec une vue directe sur le ciel étoilé ?

El club se caracteriza por habitaciones espaciosas. Y ¿qué resulta más hermoso que sumergirse en el reino de los sueños mirando directamente a las estrellas?

Open air dining while watching a magnificent sunset makes the evening hours magical. In the Grand Royal Suite, you can even view this extravaganza in an intimate atmosphere.

Open-Air zu Schlemmen mit dem Lichtspiel der untergehenden Sonne verzaubert die abendlichen Stunden. In der Grand Royal Suite gibt es dieses Schauspiel zudem in intimer Atmosphäre.

La soirée peut se transformer en un spectacle magique lorsque l'on dîne en plein air devant le spectacle lumineux du soleil couchant. Dans la suite Grand Royal, ce spectacle peut même être observé en toute intimité.

Una opípara comida al aire libre con el juego de luces de la puesta de sol embrujan las horas nocturnas. La suite Grand Royal presenta este espectáculo en una atmósfera íntima por añadidura.

Danai Beach Resort
Chalkidiki, Greece

Halfway along the sparsely populated cliffs towering above the middle finger of the Chalkidiki peninsula, at the foot of the steep, red cliffs, looms the Danai Beach Resort, surrounded by pine forests and lush gardens. It serves as a hideaway and Mediterranean sanctuary, sheltering guests far from the bustling tourist centres in an enclosed refuge of sandy beach, sea, and azure skies. In the network of the expansive grounds, songbirds or squirrels are more likely to get lost than are curious strangers. The diverse accommodations, suites and villas usually feature their own pool on the terrace, although the beach and sea are very close. Neoclassical elegance, soft and warm colors, and transparent room situations characterize the ambience of this resort.

Auf halber Strecke entlang der kaum besiedelten Steilküste, die sich über den mittleren Finger der Halbinsel Chalkidiki erstreckt, thront am Fuße der abschüssigen roten Felsen, umgeben von Pinienwäldern und üppigen Gärten, das Danai Beach Resort. Ein Hideaway und mediterranes Idyll, das seinen Gästen fern umtriebiger Ferienzentren ein in sich geschlossenes Refugium von Sandstrand, Meer und azurblauem Himmel erschließt. In das Geflecht der weitläufigen Anlage verirren sich eher Singvögel oder Eichhörnchen als neugierige Fremde. Die diversen Unterkünfte, Suiten und Villen locken zumeist mit einem eigenen Pool auf der Terrasse, obwohl Strand und Meer zum Greifen nahe sind. Neoklassische Eleganz, eine lichte wie warme Farbwelt und transparente Raumsituationen bestimmen das Ambiente des Resorts.

Le long de la côte escarpée peu habitée, à mi-chemin entre les extrémités du prolongement central de la presqu'île de Chalkidiki, trône le Danai Beach Resort au pied de falaises rouges à-pic, entouré de forêts de pins et de jardins opulents. C'est un lieu réfugié, une idylle méditerranéenne, qui offre à ses visiteurs un lieu de vacances reculé, un refuge fermé au monde extérieur, comprenant des plages de sable, la mer et un ciel au bleu d'azur. Dans la végétation de ce vaste centre, on a plus de chance de rencontrer des oiseaux qui chantent ou des écureuils que des étrangers curieux. Les divers logements, suites et villas invitent leurs invités à flâner dans la piscine privée de leur terrasse, même si la plage et la mer se trouvent à proximité. Une élégance néoclassique, des teintes claires et chaudes ainsi que des arrangements de pièces transparents caractérisent l'atmosphère du lieu.

A mitad de camino a lo largo de un acantilado apenas poblado, que se extiende sobre el dedo corazón de la península Chalkidiki, el complejo Danai Beach reina a los pies de las rocas rojas escarpadas y rodeado de bosques de pinos y jardines suntuosos. Un lugar de aislamiento y paraje mediterráneo idílico que hace inferir a los clientes de centros vacacionales remotos y enervantes la existencia de un refugio con arena de playa, mar y cielo celeste cerrado en sí mismo. En el entramado del vasto recinto se extravían antes los pájaros cantores o las ardillas que los curiosos extraños. Los diversos alojamientos, suites y mansiones atraen principalmente cuando van acompañados de una piscina propia en la terraza, a pesar de que la playa y el mar se encuentran a tiro de piedra. El ambiente del complejo se halla marcado por una elegancia neoclásica, una luz con cálido colorido y situaciones espaciales transparentes.

Pine trees lend protection and shade to the grounds, even on the terraces.

Pinien spenden der Anlage Schutz und Schatten, auch auf den Terrassen.

Les pins protègent et procurent de l ombre jusque sur les terrasses.

Los pinos proveen al recinto de protección y sombras, también en las terrazas.

From sofa to pool. Classical elegance characterizes the open rooms of this holiday accommodation.

Vom Sofa direkt in den Pool. Klassische Eleganz bestimmt die offen angelegten Räume dieses Feriendomizils.

Du canapé à la piscine ; l'élégance classique est caractérisée par les pièces très ouvertes de ce lieu de villégiature.

Directamente a la piscina desde el sofa. La elegancia clásica caracteriza las habitaciones con carácter abierto de este recinto vacacional.

Belvedere Hotel

Mykonos, Greece

Elegant dreams in blue and white? This former manor house on Mykonos, reigning over the vast panorama of the white sea of houses of Chora, is one sight that is not just an illusion. The original, meandering architecture of the property harmoniously combines the traditional with the modern, joining romantic nooks with expressively contemporary style and lifestyle. The complex, consisting of several staggered buildings, contains a total of only 41 rooms, 6 of which are suites, each with their own individual design. Each room possesses its own outdoor lounge for cosy moments. Those seeking more activity will find plenty of enticements and contacts around the winding pool, surrounded by a bar, a lounge complete with an open fireplace, restaurant and spa. This refreshing blend of old and new, of a return to Mediterranean vivacity, a sense of taste and familiar charm, all contributes to the atmosphere of the hotel, supported and lived out by its long-standing family owners.

Chice Träume in Blau und Weiß? Zu denen, die kein Trugbild bleiben, gehört dieser alte Herrensitz auf Mykonos, der mit einem weiten Blick über dem weißen Häusermeer von Chora thront. Die ursprüngliche, verwinkelte Architektur der Anlage verbindet auf harmonische Weise Tradition mit Moderne, vereint romantische Winkel mit betont jungem Stil und Lifestyle. In mehreren versetzt angeordneten Gebäudekomplexen warten insgesamt nur 41 Zimmer, davon 6 Suiten, die allesamt individuell gestaltet sind. Jede Unterkunft besitzt eine eigene Freiluft-Lounge für kuschelige Momente. Wer es belebter mag, findet Anreize und Kontakte en masse im Leben um den sich windenden Pool, gesäumt von Bar, Lounge mit Feuerstelle, Restaurant und Spa. Dieser wohltuende Einklang von alt und neu, von Rückzug und mediterraner Lebendigkeit, von Sinn für Geschmack und familiärem Charme prägt insgesamt die Atmosphäre des Hauses, getragen und vorgelebt von einer alteingesessenen Betreiberfamilie.

Avez-vous des rêves de luxe en bleu et blanc ? Cette ancienne maison de maître sur Mykonos, qui trône au dessus d'une mer blanche de maisons de la chora, n'est pas une façade trompeuse. L'architecture d'origine des bâtiments avec de nombreux angles réunit harmonieusement tradition et style moderne, angles romantiques et style jeune et « Life ». Dans les divers bâtiments décalés les uns par rapport aux autres, 41 chambres au total sont à la disposition des visiteurs, dont 6 suites, décorées dans un style personnalisé. Chaque unité de logement comprend une salle de séjour en plein air pour les instants calins. Ceux qui préfèrent la vie animée, trouveront de nombreux contacts et idées dans l'ambiance créée autour de la piscine à méandres entourée d'un bar, d'une salle de séjour avec cheminée, d'un restaurant et d'un Spa. Cette union entre l'ancien et le moderne, un lieu retiré et une vie méditerranéenne animée, un bon sens du goût et un charme familier sont les caractéristiques de l'atmosphère de la maison qui règne et qui est vécue en exemple par une famille d'hôteliers de tradition.

¿Sueños agradables en azul y blanco? Esta vieja casa señorial en Mykonos, cuyo reino se extiende más allá de una lejana mirada sobre el mar de casas blancas de Chora, pertenece a aquellos que no han quedado relegados a fantasmas. La original arquitectura angulada de la edificación enlaza de forma armoniosa tradición y modernidad, une perspectivas románticas con estilos y formas de vida con acento jovial. En varios complejos del edificio desplazados entre sí esperan un total de 41 habitaciones, 6 de ellas suites, estructuradas individualmente. Cada habitación posee su propio lounge al aire libre para momentos íntimos. Quien desee mayor actividad puede encontrar estimulación y contactos suficientes en el ambiente que gira en torno a la piscina serpenteante, bordeada por el bar, lounge con hogar, restaurante y balneario. Esta agradable armonía de antigüedad y modernidad, de aislamiento y vivacidad mediterránea, de sentido por el gusto y encanto familiar caracteriza el ambiente de la casa en su globalidad, administrada y ocupada previamente por una familia que la gestionó y permaneció en la misma durante mucho tiempo.

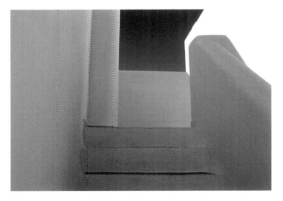

Cool places, clear lines, a dominant white, and the wind tugging at the protective sailcloths. Refreshing moments at the Belvedere.

Kühle Orte, klare Linien, dazu ein dominantes Weiß und der Wind, der mit schützenden Segeltüchern spielt. Erfrischende Momente im Belvedere.

La fraîcheur des lieux, des lignes claires, une couleur dominante: le blanc, et le vent qui fait flotter les voiles de protection. Des moments rafraîchissants au Belvedere.

Frescos lugares, líneas claras, acompañadas de una blancura dominante y el viento que juega con las lonas de protección. Refrescantes momentos en Belvedere.

On the verandas of the Belvedere, shade provides hours of relief at any time of the day. Not to mention the fascinating view.

Auf den Veranden des Belvedere spendet der Schatten zu jeder Tageszeit Stunden der Erholung. Vom faszinierenden Blick gar nicht erst zu sprechen.

Sur les vérandas du Belvedere, l'ombre est présente à toute heure de la journée et procure le repos, sans oublier le panorama fascinant.

En las terrazas del hotel Belvedere, las sombras muestran su carácter dadivoso regalando horas para el descanso en cualquier momento del día, sin siquiera mencionar las fascinantes vistas.

The restaurant, whose wine list alone boasts 5,000 entries, offers an opulent selection. Yet the architecture of the former manor house, too, dazzles both the eyes and senses.

Das Restaurant bietet allein mit 5.000 Positionen auf der Weinkarte eine opulente Auswahl. Aber auch die Architektur des alten Herrensitzes beeindruckt Augen und Sinne.

Le restaurant procure un vaste choix avec ses 5.000 offres sur la carte des vins. Mais également les yeux et les autres sens seront ravis par l'architecture de cette ancienne maison de maître.

Con 5.000 posiciones en la carta de vinos, el restaurante ofrece una suculenta selección. Pero también impresiona a la vista y los sentidos la arquitectura de la vieja casa señorial.

Almyra
Pafos, Cyprus

Cyprus is not necessarily the most well-known place to spend a holiday in the Mediterranean region. However those that pay a visit to Almyra, will come to love the island. The luxury resort by the sea provides comfort, good service and catering at the highest level. Conceived as a beach hotel which has been completely renovated, the house is surrounded by the sea, the sun and light from all sides. In addition to the two pools, as from now, guests can enjoy beauty treatments in the brand new spa area in the Almyra. For those especially fond of culinary delights there are three restaurants to spoil your palette serving international and Greek cuisine.

Zypern ist nicht unbedingt der bekannteste Ort für einen Urlaubsaufenthalt in der Mittelmeer-Region. Wer jedoch dem Almyra einen Besuch abstattet, wird die Insel lieben lernen. Das Luxus-Resort am Meer bietet Komfort, Service und Verpflegung für die höchsten Ansprüche. Als Strandhotel konzipiert und ganz neu renoviert, umgibt sich das Haus mit Meer, Sonne und Licht. Neben zwei Pools genießen die Gäste ab sofort auch die Beauty-Behandlungen im neuen Spa-Bereich des Almyras. Für Feinschmecker interessant: drei Restaurants verwöhnen mit internationalen und griechischen Speisen.

La Chypre n'est certainement pas l'endroit le plus populaire pour passer ses vacances dans la région méditerranéenne. Néanmoins, juste quelques jours de séjour à l'Almyra suffiront à tout un chacun pour découvrir son amour pour l'île. Ce complexe de luxe situé au bord de la mer offre un confort, un service et une restauration qui satisfera aux exigences les plus rigoureuses. Conçu comme hôtel de plage et entièrement rénové tout récemment, l'établissement est entouré de la mer, du soleil et de la lumière. Outre les deux piscines, les hôtes pourront dès à présent profiter des traitements de beauté offerts dans la nouvelle zone de spa de l'Almyra. Très intéressant pour les gourmets : trois restaurants vous combleront de délices internationaux et grecs.

Chipre no es precisamente el lugar más conocido para pasar unas vacaciones en la región del Mediterráneo, pero quien haga una visita al Almyra empezará a sentir cariño por la isla. El complejo de lujo situado en el mar ofrece comodidad, servicio y alimentación para las demandas más exigentes. Concebido como hotel de playa y restaurado por completo, el complejo está rodeado por el mar, el sol y la luz. Junto a las dos piscinas, los clientes ya pueden disfrutar también de los tratamientos de belleza ofrecidos en la nueva zona del balneario del Almyra. Interesante para gastrónomos: Existen tres restaurantes que le regalarán el paladar con platos internacionales y griegos.

Right by the sea, surrounded by sun—Almyra is a chic holiday resort.

Direkt am Meer, umgeben von Sonne – das Almyra ist ein schickes Urlaubs-Resort.

Juste au bord de la mer, entouré du soleil – l'Almyra est un complexe de vacances très chic.

Junto al mar y rodeado de sol, el Almyra es un atractivo complejo vacacional.

As part of the redesign: many calm areas were created in the open.

Im Zuge der Neugestaltung wurden viele Ruhezonen im Freien geschaffen.

Un grand nombre de zones de repos ont été créés dans le cadre de la reconstruction de l'établissement.

En el marco de su nuevo diseño se habilitaron muchas zonas tranquilas al aire libre.

The hotel area built in 1973 has been completely modernized. All the rooms are puritanical, bright and equipped with many seating facilities.

Die 1973 errichtete Hotelanlage ist grundlegend modernisiert worden. Alle Zimmer sind nun puristisch, hell und mit vielen Sitzgelegenheiten ausgestattet.

Le complexe hôtelier, érigé en 1973, a été entièrement modernisé. Toutes les chambres sont maintenant puristes, claires et offrent beaucoup de sièges.

El recinto hotelero abierto en 1973 se ha modernizado básicamente. Todas las habitaciones son ahora puristas, luminosas y se hallan provistas de numerosos equipamientos de cetegoría.

Index

Russia

St. Petersburg

Hotel Astoria
39 Bolshaya Morskaya Str., 190000 St. Petersburg
T +7 (812) 313 5757, F +7 (812) 313 5059
www.astoria.spb.ru

223 rooms including 29 suites. Davidov's Russian restaurant. The Bar, Borsalino Brasserie in the adjacent Angleterre Hotel, business center, 3 meeting rooms, ballroom and wintergarden hall for up to 450 persons. Fitness center, spa. Located in the heart of St. Petersburg in St. Isaac's Square.

United Kingdom

Buckinghamshire

Stoke Park Club
Park Road, Stoke Poges, Buckinghamshire SL2 4PG
T +44 (1753) 717 171, F +44 (1753) 717 181
www.stokeparkclub.com

21 bedrooms and suites. The Park Restaurant, The Orangery, The Beach Bar, 8 meeting rooms for up to 120 people. Use of the club's new Health and Racquet Pavilion (indoor swimming pool with hydro-seat jacuzzis, state-of-the-art gymnasium, multi-surface tennis courts, steam rooms, dance and fitness studios). Stoke Park Club is located 30 minutes by car from central London.

London

Knightsbridge
10 Beaufort Gardens, London SW3 1PT
T +44 (20) 7584 6300, F +44 (20) 7584 6355
www.firmdale.com

44 rooms and suites, 2 drawing rooms. Located in the heart of Knightsbridge, some minutes away from Harrods and South Kensington.

London

Threadneedles
5 Threadneedles Street, London EC2R 8AY
T +44 (20) 7657 8080, F +44 (20) 7657 8100
www.etontownhouse.com

70 rooms and suites. Restaurant and bar "Bonds", drawing room with Honesty Bar, 3 boardrooms. Situated close to the Bank of England, in the heart of the financial district only a 3 minute walk from Bank Underground Station.

The Netherlands

Amsterdam

Hotel Pulitzer
Prinsengracht 315-331, 1016 GZ Amsterdam
T +31 (20) 523 5235, F +31 (20) 627 6753
www.starwood.com/luxury

230 rooms. 8 meeting rooms for up to 160 people. Pulitzers Bar, Pulitzers Restaurant. Located near Dam Square and the Royal Palace.

Belgium

Brussels

Amigo
Rue de l'Amigo 1-3, 1000 Brussels
T +32 (2) 547 4747, F +32 (2) 513 5277
www.hotelamigo.com

177 rooms, 11 suites and Blaton-Suite with 180qm. Bar, restaurant, fitness center. Private car parking. Situated in the heart of Brussels, next to the picturesque Grand Place.

Germany

Berlin

The Regent Schlosshotel Berlin
Brahmsstraße 10, 14193 Berlin
T +49 (30) 8958 40, F +49 (30) 8958 4800
www.schlosshotelberlin.com

42 rooms, 12 suites. 3 restaurants, bar, terrace. 3 acres garden, library, meeting facilities. In Berlin Grunewald, just 5 minutes by car from Kurfürstendamm, the Internationalen Congress Center (ICC) and 12 minutes from Airport Tegel.

Burg/Spreewald

Hotel zur Bleiche
Bleichestraße 16, 03096 Burg/Spreewald
T +49 (35603) 620, F +49 (35603) 602 92
www.hotel-zur-bleiche.de

90 rooms including 7 suites, 4 suites with privat sauna/hamam. Bath house with indoor pool with fireplace, outdoor pool, spa, fitness room. 7 restaurants, meeting center for up to 150 people. Located in the heart of the Upper Spreewald.

Heiligendamm

Grand Hotel Heiligendamm
18209 Heiligendamm
T +49 (38203) 740 0, F +49 (38203) 740 7474
www.kempinski-heiligendamm.de

107 suites and 118 rooms in 6 buildings. Spa and beauty area. Golf course 5 km (9 holes), horse-riding 3 km, meeting facilities. Located on the shores of the sea, 40 km from Rostock, 2 hours from Berlin and Hamburg International Airport.

Munich

Mandarin Oriental, Munich
Neuturmstraße 1, 80331 München
T +49 (89) 290 980, F +49 (89) 222 539
www.mandarinoriental.com

73 rooms including 20 suites and junior suites. Business work station, 3 meeting rooms for up to 80 people. Restaurant Mark's, Mark's Corner, Lobby-Bar. In the historic city center within walking distance of the most attractions and elegant shops.

Switzerland

Geneva

La Réserve
301, Route de Lausanne, 1293 Genève
T +41 (22) 959 5959, F +41 (22) 959 5960
www.lareserve.ch

100 rooms and suites. Restaurant Le Tse-Fung, bar, spa. Located on the right shore of Lake Geneva, 5 km to the center of Geneva and 3 km to the International Airport of Geneva.

Lucerne

Palace Luzern
Haldenstrasse 10, 6002 Luzern
T +41 (41) 416 1616, F +41 (41) 416 1000
www.palace-luzern.ch

168 rooms and suites. Restaurant Jasper, convention and banquettes for 220 people. Within walking distance to the historical city center.

Neuchâtel

Hôtel Palafitte
2 Route des Gouttes d'Or, 2008 Neuchâtel
T +41 (32) 723 0202, F +41 (32) 723 0203
www.palafitte.ch

40 junior suites on the lakeside with private terrace, some of them with direct access to the lake. Restaurant, bar. On the shore of the Lake of Neuchâtel, 1 hour from Bern-Belp and 2,5 hours from Zurich-Kloten Airport.

Vevey

Hôtel des Trois Couronnes
49, rue d'Italie, 1800 Vevey
T +41 (21) 923 3200, F +41 (21) 923 3399
www.hoteldestroiscouronnes.com

55 rooms including 8 suites and 7 junior suites. Restaurant with panoramic terrace overlooking Lake Geneva and the Alps. Piano bar, meeting and banquete rooms for 20 to 200 people, "Puressens Spa", beauty center. 45 minutes from Geneva International Airport, 5 minutes from train station. In the heart of historical Vevey.

Austria

Vienna

Hotel Imperial
Kärntner Ring 16, 1015 Wien
T +43 (1) 501 100, F +43 (1) 5011 0410
www.starwood.com/luxury

138 rooms, 32 suites. 7 meeting rooms for up to 480 people. Maria Theresia Bar, Imperial Restaurant, Café Imperial. Near by Museum of Fine Arts, Spanish Riding School and Hofburg Convention Center.

France

Paris

Plaza Athénée
25, Avenue Montaigne, 75008 Paris
T +33 (1) 5367 6665, F +33 (1) 5367 6666
www.plaza-athenee-paris.com

106 rooms, 81 suites. 3 restaurants, Gourmet restaurant Plaza Athénée run by Alain Ducasse. Fitness center. Located in the city center, 10 minutes from Arc de Triomphe and Eiffel Tower, 30 km from Charles-de-Gaulle Airport.

Paris

Le Dokhan's
117, Rue Lauriston, 75016 Paris
T +33 (1) 5365 6699, F +33 (1) 5365 6688

45 rooms including 4 suites, restaurant, bar. Located in the city center, 10 minutes to Eiffel Tower, 30 km to Charles-de-Gaulle Airport.

Uchaux

Château de Massillan
Chemin Hauteville, 84100 Uchaux
T +33 (490) 406 451, F +33 (490) 406 385
www.chateau-de-massillan.com

20 rooms and suites, restaurant. Situated in the heart of the famous Côtes-du-Rhône wine region.

Italy

Como

Villa d'Este
Via Regina, 40, 22012 Como
T +39 (031) 348 1, F +39 (031) 348 844
www.villadeste.com

161 rooms and suites. 4 reception rooms up to 400 guests, 9 meeting rooms. Indoor pool and 2 outdoor pools. Wellness facilities, squash courts. The sporting club is directly connected to the Cardinal Villa. 18 holes Golf Club Villa d'Este 7 miles from the Hotel. The hotel is surrounded by 10 acres private park, direct access to the Lake of Como. On the shore of the Lake of Como, 67 km to Malpensa Intl. Airport.

Florence

Villa San Michele
Via Doccia, 4, 50014 Firenze
T +39 (055) 567 8200, F+39 (055) 567 8250
www.villasanmichele.orient-express.com

21 rooms, 24 suites and junior suites with private garden and terrace. Outdoor swimming pool, gym, banquet facilities. 3 restaurants, 3 bars. Located on the way up to Fiesole, only a few minutes from the center of Florence.

Gargnano

Villa Feltrinelli
Via Rimembranza 38-40, 25084 Gargnano
T +39 (0365) 798 000, F +39 (0365) 798 001
www.villafeltrinelli.com

21 rooms and suites, "Boat House" with private landing stage, swimming pool, library, open fireside, privat dining room. Situated on the western shore of the Lake Garda.

Milan

Four Seasons Hotel Milano
Via Gesù 8, 20121 Milano
T +39 (02) 7708 8, F +39 (02) 7708 5000
www.fourseasons.com/milan

118 rooms including 41 suites. 2 restaurants, foyer lounge, business center, conference facilities for up to 300 guests. Fitness center. Located in the city center, within walking distance to Piazza al Duomo and La Scala Opera, 45 minutes from Malpensa International Airport.

Perugia

Brufani Palace
Piazza Italia 12, 06100 Perugia
T +39 (075) 573 2541, F +39 (075) 572 0210
www.sinahotels.com

94 rooms including 31 suites. Indoor swimming pool, fitness room. Restaurants, 2 bars and meeting facilities. Located in the city center, 15 minutes to Perugia Airport, 2,15 hours to Rome Fumicino International Airport.

Rome

Hotel de Russie
Via del Babuino 9, 00187 Roma
T +39 (06) 3288 81, F +39 (06) 3288 8888
www.hotelderussie.it

129 bedrooms including 24 suites. Restaurant Le Jardin du Russie, Stravinskij Bar. 5 function suites for 10 to 100 people. Health spa and beauty salon. Close to the Spanish Steps and Piazza del Popolo.

Venice

Bauer Venezia
San Marco 1459, 30124 Venezia
T +39 (041) 520 7022, F +39 (041) 520 7557
www.bauervenezia.com

96 rooms, 21 suites. 2 restaurants, meeting facilities for small meetings. Il Palazzo at the Bauer: 35 palatial rooms, 40 suites. Gourmet restaurant "De Pisis" with terrace on the Grand Canal, "Settimo Cielo" terrace and lounge on the 7th floor with view over the city. Located in the historical center.

Venice

Danieli
Castello 4196, 30122 Venezia
T +39 (041) 522 6480, F +39 (041) 520 0208
www.starwood.com/luxury

192 double rooms, 29 single rooms, 12 suites and junior suites. Restaurant, bar, banqueting rooms for up to 350 persons. Private beach and sporting facilities on Venice Lido. Only steps away from the Piazza San Marco, the Basilica di San Marco, the Doge's Palace and the Bridge of Sighs.

Venice

San Clemente Palace
Isola di San Clemente 1, 30124 Venezia
T +39 (41) 244 5001, F +39 (41) 244 5800
www.sanclemente.thi.it

205 rooms and suites. 6 conference rooms for up to 450 people. 4 restaurants. Tennis courts, golf course, beauty & wellness club. Perched on a private Venetian Island overlooking Piazza San Marco, Guidecca and the Lido. 10 minutes by private boat shuttle from Piazza San Marco.

Portugal

Madeira

Choupana Hills Resort & Spa
Travessa do Largo da Choupana, 9050-286 Funchal
T +351 (291) 206 020, F +351 (291) 206 021
www.choupanahills.com

64 rooms including 4 suites. Xôpana Restaurant, bars and lounge. Health and beauty spa, turkish bath, sauna, jacuzzi, indoor and outdoor pool. On the hills overlooking Funchal and the ocean. 20 minutes from the airport.

Lisbon

Palácio Belmonte
Páteo Dom Fradique 14, 1100 - 624 Lisboa
T +351 (21) 881 6600, F +351 (21) 881 6609
www.palaciobelmonte.com

8 suites. 2 libraries with more than 4000 books. Business club, small chapel, swimming pool. Located in the heart of Lisbon.

Spain

Barcelona

Gran Hotel La Florida
Carretera de Vallvidrera al Tibidabo 83-93, 8035 Barcelona
T. +34 (93) 259 3000, F. +34 (93) 259 3001
www.hotellaflorida.com

52 rooms, 22 suites, some of the rooms with private jacuzzi. Restaurant, bar. Spa and beauty center, indoor and outdoor swimming pool, gym. Located on Mount Tibidabo, views over the city and the Mediterranean Sea. 20 minutes to the city center, 1/2 hour from the airport.

Madrid

Hesperia
Paseo de la Castellana 57, 28046 Madrid
T +34 (91) 210 8800, F +34 (91) 210 8899
www.hesperia-madrid.com

137 rooms, 34 suites, suites with butler service. Gourmet restaurant "Santceloni" run by Santi Santamaria. restaurant and 2 bars, meeting facilities. Located in the business district, 8 km from Madrid Barajas Airport.

Marbella

Rio Real Golf Hotel
Urbanización Río Real, 29600 Marbella
T +34 (952) 765 732, F+34 (952) 772 140
www.rioreal.com

16 rooms, 14 suites. Meeting facilities, 2 restaurants, 2 bars. Outdoor swimming pool. 18 hole golf course.

Mallorca

Ca's Xorc
Carretera de Deia, km 56.1, 07100 Sóller
T +34 (971) 638 280, F +34 (971) 632 949
www.casxorc.com

13 rooms, 1 restaurant, pool with panoramic view and large private garden. Located in the hills above Port Sóller, 40 minutes from Palma de Mallorca and the airport.

Seville

Hotel Alfonso XIII
San Fernando 2, 41004 Sevilla
T +34 (95) 491 7000, F +34 (95) 491 7099
www.westin.com/hotelalfonso

146 rooms including 19 suites. Sevillian inner courtyard with fountain "El Patio", San Fernando Bar, poolside snack-bar (open in summer). 7 splendid function rooms. Located in the historical city center, near the banks of the Guadalquivir river and only minutes away from the Cathedral, The Plaza de España, the Toro del Oro and the Reales Alcazares.

Greece

Athens

Grand Resort Lagonissi
40 km Athens-Sounio Ave., 19010 Lagonissi
T +30 (22910) 760 00, F +30 (22910) 245 34
www.lagonissiresort.gr

188 rooms including 50 suites. 7 restaurants, bars, clubs, meeting rooms for up to 300 people. Located 40 km from the center of Athens, 20 km from Venizelos International Airport.

Chalkidiki

Danai Beach Resort
Nikiti, 63088 Chalkidiki
T +30 (23750) 223 10, F +30 (23750) 225 91
www.danai-beach.gr

Spacious villas with 61 rooms and 54 suites, 13 of them with private pool. Fitness room, pool, tennis court. Restaurants: The Pavillon, (sea view restaurant), The Squirrel (open air), The Sea Horse Grill, The Sea Side Bar, The Pool Bar. 50 minutes from Thessaloniki airport.

Mykonos

Belvedere Hotel
School of Fine Arts District, 84600 Mykonos
T +30 (2289) 0 251 22, F +30 (2289) 0 251 26
www.belvederehotel.com

47 rooms including 6 suites. Restaurant, snack bar, pool bar. Fitness studio, massage therapy, spa therapy services. 5 minutes walking distance to the center of the island.

Cyprus

Pafos

Almyra
P.O. Box 60136, 8125 Pafos
T +357 (26) 933 091, F +357 (26) 942 818
www.thanoshotels.com/paphos/pbhfrm.html

190 rooms. Walking distance to the castle and close to the House of Dionysos with its stunning mosaics.

Photo Credits

Babylon Design London	Château de Massillan	96
Roland Bauer	Threadneedles	28
	Grand Hotel Heiligendamm	48
	Plaza Athénée	84
	Le Dokhan's	90
	Four Seasons Hotel Milano	120
	Bauer Venezia	138
	San Clemente Palace	150
	Villa d'Este	3, 102
	Brufani Palace	3, 126
	Palace Luzern	3, 64
Carlos Cezanne	Palácio Belmonte	164
Firmdale Hotels	Knightsbridge	11, 22
Oberto Gili	Villa Feltrinelli	112
Manuel Gomes da Costa	Palácio Belmonte	164
Helios Hotels	Grand Resort Lagonissi	196
Hesperia somo hoteleros	Hesperia	174
Rainer Hofmann	Mandarin Oriental, Munich	54
Martin Nicholas Kunz	Mandarin Oriental, Munich	54
	Hôtel Palafitte	70
	Hôtel des Trois Couronnes	74
	Hotel de Russie	132
	Choupana Hills Resort & Spa	156
	Palácio Belmonte	164
	Gran Hotel La Florida	168
	Ca's Xorc	186
	La Réserve	3, 58
Yvan Moreau	La Réserve	58

Orient-Express Hotels	Villa San Michele	108
Ana Paula	Palácio Belmonte	164
Izar Perliman	Palácio Belmonte	164
Mauro Ranzoni	Four Seasons Hotel Milano	4, 120
Simone Reggiori	Villa Feltrinelli	112
courtesy Roccoforte Hotels	Amigo	36
	Hotel de Russie	132
	Hotel Astoria	3, 7, 12
courtesy Starwood, Westin Hotels	Hotel Pulitzer	32
	Hotel Imperial	80
	Danieli	146
	Hotel Alfonso XIII	192
Thanos Hotels	Almyra	2, 212
Henry Thoureau	Villa Feltrinelli	112
Ottavio Tomasini	Villa Feltrinelli	112
courtesy Villa Feltrinelli	Villa Feltrinelli	Cover, 8
T. Vrettus	Belvedere Hotel	2, 206, Backcover
Other photos, courtesy		
	Stoke Park Club	18
	The Regent Schlosshotel	40
	Hotel zur Bleiche	44
	Ca's Xorc	186
	Danai Beach Resort	202
	Choupana Hills Resort & Spa	2, 156
	Rio Real Golf Hotel	2, 180

Editor Martin Nicholas Kunz

Editorial coordination Patricia Massó

Introduction Professor Axel Müller-Schöll

Hotel texts by Bärbel Holzberg, Frank Bantle (riva medien), Benjamin A. Finn, Anja Schimanke, Melanie Erkens, Inna Hartwich, Heinfried Tacke & Martin Nicholas Kunz

Layout & Prepress Markus Mutz

Translations AdeTeam
English: Dr. Andrea Adelung, Vineeta Manglani
French: Eric Lingo, Christine Seguret
Spanish: Miguel Carazo

Published by teNeues Publishing Group

teNeues Publishing Company
16 West 22nd Street, New York, NY 10010, US
Tel.: 001-212-627-9090, Fax: 001-212-627-9511

teNeues Verlag GmbH + Co. KG
Book Division
Kaistraße 18
40221 Düsseldorf, Germany
Tel.: 0049-(0)211-994597-0, Fax: 0049-(0)211-994597-40

teNeues Publishing UK Ltd.
P.O. Box 402
West Byfleet
KT14 7ZF, Great Britain
Tel.: 0044-1932-403509, Fax: 0044-1932-403514

teNeues France S.A.R.L.
4, rue de Valence
75005 Paris, France
Tel.: 0033-1-55765205, Fax: 0033-1-55766419

www.teneues.com

© 2003 teNeues Publishing Group

ISBN: 3-8238-4553-5

Printed in Germany